Olive Branch

Joy Comes in the Morning

Simone Faith

Olive Branch

Published by Revival Waves of Glory Books & Publishing

PO Box 596| Litchfield, Illinois 62056 USA

www.revivalwavesofgloryministries.com

Published in the United States of America

ISBN 978-0692659014

Table of Contents

Acknowledgments 4

Prologue 5

Chapter 1 Can Sinners Enter? 6

Chapter 2 Idle Words 19

Chapter 3 The Entrance 22

Chapter 4 Worshipping False Idols 29

Chapter 5 One God 36

Chapter 6 What If 41

Chapter 7 The Greatest Is Love 52

Chapter 8 Thank You! 55

Chapter 9 His Holy Place 57

Chapter 10 God Loves You If No One Else Does 59

Grace 63

Acknowledgments

This project has required the help of many people. My first thanks must go to God, for he knew the plans for my life before I was born. A thank you goes out to my Grand-Mother who has been gone a long time, I thank her for everything she has done. I thank my late friend Stephanie White, who was a friend to the very end. This book is also dedicated to the many people who I have encountered that have changed my life, if I have missed anybody I apologize. I also want to thank my publisher Bill Vincent who gave me a chance. Last but certainly not least, I want to thank my husband Anthony and my five children for always believing this project could happen.

Prologue

I'm still here while the others were taken, what happened? I began to shake, I cried for help, but everyone was crying. The world was in confusion, people were jumping from burning buildings, looting was everywhere, accidents were all around. The sky was filled with darkness. People were shouting, "It happened," while others were on their knees asking for forgiveness. I had no idea the true impact this would have. I believed in Jesus, I thought I had time. I thought I could keep living as I pleased. I believed all my good deeds would save me. I watched the buildings fall as I yelled with fear people began to run, but had nowhere to hide. I saw what I thought was the anti-Christ, as he grabs them all. People were pleading the blood of Jesus but were beheaded. The Bible spoke the truth, I chose to ignore it and now I fight to live...

Chapter 1

Can Sinners Enter?

The room is dark I can't see a thing, with his hands all over my body. It feels good, sometimes I wish this was my husband. We both belong to someone else. His large hands grasp every part of my body, I feel like a woman. My body yearns for more, it may be wrong, but I crave the affection of real love. My heart beats faster with every touch. It seems so right.

My husband is cold and distant, and we have fallen apart. Our love has faded. I can't remember the last time he said I was beautiful, he works seven days a week, we go months without affection. His devices have become his life. For years I dreamed of another man loving me the way I wanted to be loved, I even thought of meeting people online. I can't remember the last time he held me or even said he loved me. We argue all the time over petty things. One time we argued over a wine display in the kitchen, and this was enough to have him sleep on the couch for three weeks. I don't know where we went wrong. Here I am now Thirty-Two married to a man who is ten years my junior, am I the pedophile? there was a secret part of me who wanted to make him the man I wanted him to be not the man he would soon become.

I ask myself was I leaving my husband for the wrong man? He knows I'm married, but he doesn't care. He says my husband won't find out, if he does Will he even care?

Let me start from the beginning my name is Faith my husband is Josh. When we met he was handsome, I thought he was the ideal man. He opened doors, and was built like an athlete. I thought we would be together forever, but there was one problem I was dating other people from the beginning.

People said it wouldn't last, they said what you give is what you get. We were young, so it didn't matter. We thought it was forever. I cheated all ten years of our marriage, and so did he. I even cheated in our bed where we lay our heads. He cheated, but for all the wrong reasons, he was young and curious, I was always looking for the next best thing. I found love in everyone's bed, except my husband. I was a good liar, never once have I admitted to being married. I could say I was at work and my husband would believe it. The more things I found out about him, the more things I did.

Sex, it was good with everyone but my husband. This person was always better than the next. What was I doing? My marriage was falling apart; I knew it was wrong. Yet I was afraid to leave, I had kids. I was taught to stand by your man, that's what a good wife does and that's what I did. My husband cheated on internet sites time after time, he even had family members help him.

In the beginning when he cheated It felt sickening like I couldn't compare to these women. I was so tired of dealing with all the secrets, but then again I was stuck, I needed his money. We had a big home, fancy cars, we were living a good but he wasn't attracted to me. Did I become too fat? I couldn't figure it out, I soon began to pray. I felt like God had stopped listening. It wasn't long before I started going back to church, now church was something I now loathed.

I didn't hate church, like most. With the help of my Grandmother I went to church even when she didn't. I just hated the fakes, and I was fake. I didn't want to come to God unless I was going to be real not to mention I was angry with him, I always knew about God, but could he really change me? did he even care about a sinner like me?

while I was cheating Josh was too. One day I found pornography books and they were all in Japanese Cartoon He was secretly on dating sites saying his relationship was complicated while being my husband; I had no regrets being with another man. I would like to say I did, but I didn't. It was easy to fall for someone who act like I was important, while Josh did things in the dark, I did mine in the open. Josh entire family knew he was having affairs, his mother helped him secretly divorce me. Yes, you read that right, we were divorced for a year before we got back together. One day he came home while I was pregnant and divorced me, I couldn't cry I didn't want to be his wife anymore. I was happy when I thought he was gone, but we got back together. I can't even tell you why I had no idea the effect this would have on me, or my family until they grew up.

I saw how dysfunctional my children were, they couldn't hold relationships, they were afraid of commitments, some hated women, and mostly they hated him, they felt like he was a foe, not a father. I can't even really say he liked kids I think he pretended to. He started doing things when I wasn't there like cursing at the kids or spanking them. I stayed in the middle. I knew I had a big part in how my children life turned out, I just couldn't admit it. I mean what mother wants to admit she's lousy, what mother wants to admit she's wrong? as a child almost every kid feels they could have had a better life and I was no exception to the rule. If you are a parent and have two children, one goes to college and the other becomes a crack head or winds up in jail does that make you the bad parent or the child a bad kid?

One Saturday I had a dream that I went to church, while in church the pastor was talking about the coming of Jesus. Well all of a sudden the rapture happens and I was left behind, I woke up and it was Sunday morning. I told my husband and he laughed. I then said let's just go to church. I mean I am a sinner look at all the stuff I've done; why would God be talking to me. I took the kids and my husband and While in church the preacher spoke of the rapture, when I first heard the sermon I was a little shocked but I thought it was a coincidence even though just yesterday I had this dream, was God telling me the time has come? maybe I ate too much the night before. When I heard him I thought they have been preaching this for years and still no Jesus. Over two thousand years preachers have been saying this, when any national disaster happens people say it's the end of the world. All over YouTube everybody is a prophet, and everyone know the world is ending. I became mad, even bitter towards God, as the preacher was reading on the rapture he read that no liars, fornicators and so on would inherit the kingdom of heaven.

Well, I guess I was going straight to hell. One day at church I decided to tell the pastor the things I did while married, when I entered the church my heart felt heavy. there was a spirit in me that I couldn't explain. I wanted God to forgive me. I thought it was between my pastor and myself, I was wrong. The pastor told the Deacons and they told the Bishops. I soon left the church of embarrassment.

The whole church said I was filthy I wasn't dressed up I had no fancy hats, I was a regular Joe Blow. I came in jeans and tennis shoes, I wanted this salvation that these Christians had. I wanted to believe that Jesus could help me. I knew I was dirty, I knew I didn't live right, but that didn't stop me from wanting some help. There was nothing special about me no great education no wealthy background, just me. The congregation did nothing for me, I received snares and secret whispers, looks that made me feel like a tramp, I thought if there was a God where was he when I was hungry? There were days when mustard and sugar was my best friend. I had nobody but where was God when I needed him? I turned to the streets, and turned my back on God.

One day while partying, I met a man named Black who would eventually leave me. People say the grass is always greener on the other side, but I was eager to find out.

He was different from my husband, my husband wouldn't buy a thing unless it said clearance, sale or free. Black took me everywhere. I was on cloud nine, I wanted to have sex again, that alone was major. I'm sure there are many women who lay next to their husband and don't even think about sex, I never dreamed this would happen, I always thought when I was married, we would be in love, and he would be my protector, I was wrong. There were times we wouldn't talk, just walk around like zombies. The thought of my husband touching me made my skin crawl. You know sex was supposed to be my wifely duties, but how would I do this, I tried to fake it, but you can only do that for so long. Remember I said he was fine in the beginning, but towards the end he begins to look like a duck on crack, fat grew in places that should have stayed skinny, and places turned gray that should have stayed black, and things sag that should not! I fell in love or shall I say lust with Black. While dating black I met Summer and Tuff. Both went to my church they appeared to be the ideal couple at least from what I could tell, but you never know people. Summer and I became very close, she let me know she secretly hated her husband. I didn't want to tell her that I felt the same way, but I wondered how the church accepted her knowing she didn't love him. She only married him to leave the ghettos of south-central, now her husband was truly a man of God, he never cursed, he gave all he could and he loved his family. Unfortunately, he had the wrong wife, Tuff believed in his heart that Summer was sent from heaven. Summer was strange, every three weeks she wanted a divorce. Believe it or not I felt like God had me meet them so I could take a look at my life. She was always mad about something, come to find out she had many skeletons and they were about to come out.

Two weeks before December twenty- first I was having the time of my life. I was laughing, shopping having a good time. I bought a new car, started a new job and found a new church. All was well I met new people who seemed to like me, but something appeared to be wrong, as I walked out the mall I noticed my sunny day had changed, I thought something was wrong with my eyes, for a brief second. The sun looked as though it jumped. I took off my shades to take a second look, but then clouds started drawing at a vast rate, sunlight was soon leaving and all that was around was darkness and I wanted to hurry home. This must be a storm rolling in. The clouds had somehow covered the sun, this is going to be a massive thunderstorm I could no longer see the blue skies, the birds had disappeared, it was as if they never flew. I tried to call my husband, but I had no service, my husband always called my cell phone, "dumb phone," and this time I agreed with him since I could not reach him. I wished I had a smart phone instead of this stupid phone, I ran to my car as fast as I could, trying not to fall. Within moments rain came down, my heart calmed down as I thought this is just a thunderstorm, it seemed like I was in traffic for hours, everyone was on the road I guess we were all trying to take cover, this was odd. I looked down at my watch and noticed it was only in the afternoon, could this be the lunch rush? Of course not, silly me it was a Saturday, and the streets were packed. I forgot it was two weeks before Christmas this was a big shopping weekend, people were everywhere, I tried to call my husband this time he answered, I was so mad I began yelling.

I said, "are you looking at this rain? Why didn't you answer my call? You knew it was me." Each time he tried to talk I just said whatever, I told him, "you ought to be happy to have someone like me," you see I thought I looked better than him well I was wrong according to God, beauty really is skin deep, how could I be prettier than him when I was turning gray and fighting to stay young.

He replied, "what is that supposed to mean?"

Again, I said, "you know what I mean. You know I only got married to you so I could get out of the ghetto!" I could hear the tears in his voice, but I didn't care.

He said, "Faith I'll pray for you, I know God has a plan for us, he brought us together,"

I immediately got mad and asked, "are you at church?"

He said, "yes, I'm here in bible class."

I said, "you're always at church, here it's the storm of the century and instead of being at home, you are in church praying to a God who could care less!"

Josh replied, "Faith I will be home soon and I will ask God to forgive you."

I yelled, "I didn't need God to forgive me, you need to ask God why he gave me your broke ass!"

My husband hung up, I was left saying hello, this man hung up on me. I hung up the phone and stuck a CD in, I began to sing when all of a sudden a huge streak of lighting zoomed across the sky, it went so fast I thought I was seeing things. I came to a sudden stop as the other drivers did, I turned down the music and looked out my window. I tried to see where the lightning went, but I couldn't. I looked as far as the eye could see, still nothing. The next thing I heard was a boom it was like a sonic boom like something from the movies. I Began to see windows blow out, glass flew everywhere, people started screaming it was like a reaction to something scary, I was terrified. While sitting in traffic the buildings to my left began to shake, they swayed as if pushed over by a child, they seem to just crumble and fall. I looked and thought this has got to be a joke, an earthquake is hard to explain what was happening. What is going on, was the question running through my mind, but it shook for two minutes and it was over, I was relieved to say the least. I was only a few minutes from my home and thought if I could get there I would be safe.

We lived in Hollywood, and I loved it, all the stars were there, and so being the sinners. We were home to nightlife, now nightlife in Hollywood was different from any place in the world, by day you could shop the best places, but night gave way to something eerie and strange just the way I like it. We had events of what I like to call private mansion parties, now at these parties we did things that only special people knew about. You had to swear an oath that if anyone found out you would lie no matter what, we had people above us who would even destroy evidence to keep people safe. At these parties there was a little bit of everything from animals to drugs, even prostitutes of every kind, you name it and we had it all for a price. See in Hollywood money talks. And what do I mean by animals well, let's just say sometimes fantasy goes well beyond a threesome if you know what I mean. You could find anything you wanted to do at night, my husband hated that place he told me it reminded him of Solomon and Gomorrah, but I loved the lesbian couples, I loved the men who were the same sex, I loved the freakish hair styles and the nightclubs that had secret things you could do that nobody knew about. Hollywood truly was a don't ask, and we won't tell town policy. Hollywood had real Psychics and fake ones before the night of the twenty- first. I met a lady named Athena, she was standing outside a beautiful blue and white house, as I was walking by she told me I was married, but I was having an affair, quickly I turned around of course. This struck my interest now in my mind she was either very gifted and came from God or she was from Satan himself but either way I had to know. I walked up to her, and she looked quite normal, she asked me to stick out my palm. She told me spirits were all around me, I was scared. I didn't tell her that, but at this point I wanted to run away. She said that I had been cheating for years, but things of this world were about to change, I looked at her, she then said something really weird, she threw my hand down and said the kingdom of God is at hand, she said repent or suffer the wrath of God, then she grabs me, I tried to run, but she repeated it over and over. She then said before the week is over everyone you know will be dead! I ran fast as I could.

I came to a stop, I thought about my flaws. I found myself in a park and began to think about my husband. Josh was not a good looking man, from the moment we met I was not attracted to him, He was tall and dark as dirt, and some compared him to midnight. He looked like Lurch, I have no idea why I married him, he had no special education, and ninth grade is where he stopped. I wondered many times why God put us together we were like oil and water we just didn't mix. I learned from the women in my family that as long as a man had money, nothing mattered. Dollars seemed to rule the world. When you grow up with little, you believe the little minds of little thinkers. The problem was I couldn't predict the future. You have no idea what will become of your life. The things I was taught didn't work, I was on the same path as the women in my family either sleeping with married men, or marrying someone I didn't love. So the advice they gave got old real fast, the women in my family would say you could learn to love anybody. That's another lie and so far that wasn't working either. I thought when I was married I would have this dream house and these beautiful children and this picture perfect family. I was wrong, as I look back, I made a mistake after mistake. I gave the wrong man my body. Here I was many years later with a husband who I had no feelings for, but I couldn't afford to divorce. I asked myself what do you do when God turns a deaf ear, what happens when years go by and you hear nothing, I had this religious freak husband saying God cared but where were these miracles that God did with the leaders of the past? Was I too much of a sinner to get help? Where was God when I needed him the most? I hoped to meet someone rich, but I couldn't, how could I when I was only making seven dollars and twenty-five cents, to most of the world I was invisible I was working as a cashier no one knew me. Looks didn't pay my bills. I was in no shape to meet a person who had more, I kept my thoughts to myself. What if this Psychic was right, what if everyone I knew was going to die? I had no idea why, what had they done. Maybe I just had the look of a cheat. Lots of people cheat, maybe that was a lucky guess.

***

I made it home, one of the few times I thanked God. Once I went into my house I went to my bedroom. I looked out the big window and could see the raindrops the size of golf balls, was I mistaken? I got up to see more clearly but my vision was blurred by the curtains covering the windows. I had never seen raindrops that huge, it was hitting the windows so hard they almost shattered, the noise was so loud that with each hit my heart fluttered. Instantly I thought about what that psychic said and became nervous, never once did I get on my knees and repent.

I called my husband, but he didn't answer, I text him to see if he was on his way, I received no reply within minutes he walked through the door.

"Josh look at this rain, what is going on?" I asked.

He said, "I don't know."

I asked, "can we leave?"

He replied, "no we need to stay and pray."

"I'm not praying I don't believe in God. God has never done anything for me. Josh where was your God when I was getting molested as a little kid? Where was your God when my mother didn't want me? Where was your God when my father got my mother pregnant and ran out on us? Where was God when I needed a job?" I asked getting frustrated.

"I can't answer all those questions, but you had to go through all that for a reason," he said.

"If he is a God of love he would have helped me, he would have healed my tears, he would not have allowed me to be abused. Josh how do you explain a God who is so rich but allow his children to be so poor? I was so poor I was looking for pennies on the ground just to buy soup," I said.

Josh said, "I am sorry that happened, but bad things happen to good people all the time God is just. The sun shines on the good and the bad, God doesn't take away the sun from the bad, but he gives them a chance, you haven't given God a chance to heal you. You have to forgive; you have to forgive all those who have hurt you, and you have to let go. You hold in so much hate. If you don't let go, how can God help you? God can not lie. You will spend eternity in hell! Faith you may have gone through a lot as a child but look at your life now, you never know what God has planned for you." He said the last part with a gentle smile.

"Josh there is no way in hell I believe all that crap about a red devil with horns and burning fire."

"You are a bigger idiot than I thought", Josh replied. "God will not be mocked!" He yelled walking away.

I began to think about the things I did in secret like watch pornography, I tried to stop but I couldn't. I was addicted, it was my secret. I planned my life not knowing at this very moment it would change forever. My husband was a church going man, he prayed, he cried and day after day he told me to change my life. My husband said the world was ending, but I didn't listen, preachers have been saying this for years, I would go on YouTube and see all these people claim they were having these dreams and I would always leave these smart remarks. *Why would this happen now?* I told my husband hell is not real, that's what we say to scare people who are bad. I told him heaven might not be real, but my husband would tell me that God word is real. We argued. He yelled, "I believe in Jesus, even demons believe in Jesus."

As usual, I walked away never wanting to hear the truth. That night I was mad I went to sleep angry, my husband tried to apologize but I pretended to sleep.

Chapter 2

Idle Words

There is a passage in the bible that states for every idle word spoken men will give account in the Day of Judgment. (Matthew 12:36). When you think of idle words what do you think about? The synonym for idle is vain, and the synonym for vain is useless - Unavailing - idle - conceited – empty, but I'm sure none of these words describe you. I came across this passage and I thought about the way I talk. I say things to hurt people, I have been vengeful since birth. I was taught self-first self-last and if there is anything left let self-get it.

God is not a liar and he will not be mocked. I know that some may wonder why God would create a hell if he's an all loving God. As long as man continues to commit sin then we have to pay for it. Remember Hell was created for the angels that disobeyed God, man has decided not to believe, and to sin willfully. There is no impurity in heaven,

I often wondered why Jesus took our death? And if times were different, would we die for him? Some would but most would choose to live in the pit with the fallen angels.

Man refuse to believe that there is a second life after this one. As humans, we don't care who we hurt or why they hurt, we go about our lives as if nothing will happen. We believe we have the right to live as we please like our choices are fine.

I once had a co-worker at a business, she was a great manager, she always exceeded our daily sales, profit, but she was an awful manager on the inside. She spoke to people harshly, she talked to people like dirt, we spoke often and on a few occasions she told me she was going to heaven, I can't say whether or not she will go, certainly she will have to answer to God for how she treated people.

Another instance, was an old lady, she had been raped as a child by her stepfather, when she got old enough to leave, she harbored hate towards her mother. She waited for the day her mother grew old. She wanted her to feel the pain she endured as a child. Not only was she raped but she had a baby. By the age of twelve, she was a woman and a mother all in one. The Old lady always felt her mother should have known that her stepfather was creeping into her room, she secretly hated the child she had, she wanted nothing to do with him. She wanted revenge on her mother, soon her mother was too old to care for herself, but not before her daughter would abuse her, she fought her, when she was hungry she wouldn't feed her. When her mother had company her daughter would pull down her pants and panties, and laugh at her.

The mother cried, but felt as though she deserved it. She allowed her daughter to have her husband baby. The lady grew cold, love never lived in her heart, her mother soon died and often she cried but could not take back what had been done. She cursed out her friends, she treated people badly. She tried to buy friendships, but it never worked. People came around as long as she had money, when the money ran out so did the friends. Soon the lady became old, not much changed, she stopped going to church, and God slowly left her life. I like to call this Luke warm for God. Soon she had gotten so ill death was near the doors, she lay ill with her last breaths, each breath she took was with fear. Her last days was painful, she lay in a hospital bed, not weighing more than sixty pounds. Her hair grew long her smile weary, and her laughter faded away. At that point, I knew we were not more than a vapor. Thirst is what she craved many times before her death, she told me how thirsty she was, then it happened before she died, she had hard breaths, I don't know if she repented. I know she believed in God, but I realized that once saved is not always is true.

I was told by people who was there she sat straight, looked in a corner with fear and died. The spiritual world exists, we think these movies are fake, some things that we think exist are only in our dreams.

Idle words, I leave you with this. We all have said something, but if the souls could come back from the grave they would ask for just enough time to save their soul.

Before you say something you may regret, think about it. You can reverse time!

Chapter 3

The Entrance

It was about three a.m. when I heard what seemed to be a trumpet, my husband never woke up. I heard a third trumpet and by far this was louder than the first two.

When I looked out my window I could see people in other apartment windows as if we all woke at the same time. People began to walk outside and look in the sky. At this moment the trumpet went on four more times before I could wake my husband he disappeared. There was nothing left, nothing. I lift up the sheets to see if he was playing a game, I began to scream. I ran maybe this was an alien invasion, that's what I saw on YouTube weeks before. I tried to think of everything, I thought who would I call first? I called my mother but the phone went dead so I hung up. I called my mother in law, she was still here, I thought most of my family is here but where is my husband?

I ran up the street to Summer and Tuff's house, and I found Summer on the floor with a gun screaming saying my *husband just vanished, help me*. I didn't know what to do I just stood there, I didn't know what to say. She began rocking back and forth saying Jesus came, I laughed gently thinking she was going crazy.

I said, "Summer, your hysterical." She started reaching for the gun and put it to her head. I screamed in fear. "Wait! We'll find him," I said with a trembling voice.

Summer began looking around the room asking me can you see them? I thought my friend was losing her mind.

I asked, "see what?"

She said, "they were coming for me."

I said, "it's okay Summer put the gun down I am here."

No one was helping. People began to say the rapture happened, I didn't know for sure but I thought these people were crazy. I tried to get to the church, but the streets were so crowded I couldn't find my way. God came for his bride. I had no idea what they meant. We did not see these people go up like the movies said this would happen, I saw nothing. It happened fast, I didn't sleep I was wide awake, missed it. One minute he was sleeping the next he vanished. People who were in delivery trucks, vanished. Cars were crashing one after another. I watched planes fall, but people were not dying, Women, who were pregnant, began to scream they were no longer pregnant. Blood and tears filled the earth. People began looting in the midst of a tragedy. People ran "saying the rapture has come, God is real."

I looked up, and the clouds were the darkest I had ever seen. The clouds were moving fast I was afraid, the moon covered by a thick red circle and the stars were so close I thought they were going to fall. Birds began to hit the ground; people had taken cover. Birds fell by the hundreds and death was among the nation. I tried to remember the Lord's Prayer, but I couldn't think, I attempted to pray, but I heard a voice say it's too late. It's too late, I could hear the tears of Jesus weeping in the many souls that were going to hell. I ran back to the house and turned on the TV.

The news was telling people all over the world people had vanished at three in the morning by the millions. They tried to say it was an alien abduction, and this went on for hours. I turned off my TV. I knew this was the rapture. I began to think of all the times my pastor told me to change, and how the time was at hand. I started to think of all the bad things I had done and how I kept saying tomorrow, and now tomorrow was here. I thought of all the times I was in church and how many times I ignored God call I tried to maintain, but I could not, God took my husband, my ten-year-old and my six-year-old. I began to think do kids go to hell? Right now I'm sure they do. Once they know the difference between good and evil they must choose.

Jesus is a gentleman he does not make you serve him it's a choice. I use to think it was by force. That was my sad mistake, many tried to get me to believe, but I wouldn't, you see it's hard to believe in something you can't see. My two boys woke up, and they saw me crying they asked what happened, I told them daddy, and everyone else went to heaven, we were left here. Both my sons began to cry. I thought about my children's life, my youngest was a thief, and a liar any given time he would steal or take something that did not belong to him. He had no respect for my husband or me. My oldest wanted to fight the world, he claimed he was only a Christian because of me. He hated everyone and everybody. He also never wanted to help. He used people, we were all fake Christians. Going to church on Sundays and living in the world during the week.

But God says be not of this world lest ye be transformed. I finally know what that means. If you act like the people who sin in this world, then you too will pay for your sins. For years, I went to church, but never understood the meaning. The word comes by faith and faith from hearing the word of God. I write these things to you brother and sister so that you might be saved. When these things happened, it came with a shock, I was not expecting it, I know what the word says but I tell you the truth I was preparing my lamp in the dark.

My children and I walked outside, we heard a thump like a blowing of a loud instrument, something that would scare you when you first hear it, something that would make you stand still. Something that was loud it shook the ground.

The Thump was so loud that it scared us out the mist of people disappearing before the earth shook. I looked up in the sky and great beings as I have never seen came out the sky, they were coming through trees, the trees were nothing compared to these things. Men and women could not run fast enough to get out their way, children were trampled. They died in front of their parents. These things looked like something from a horror movie, as if the worst horror movie had come alive. They were eating people's flesh and killing people. These things were the lost souls of hell, they were happy that God's protection was off the world. Everyone was running, people were leaving their children. I ran to a building, and I went under dead bodies I told my sons to follow, my youngest son, was caught and killed. I watched in horror as this thing ripped his head off and threw it for miles, this thing had eight wings and only two eyes, he was at least thirty feet he could smell as good as a dog. It was hard to hide myself and my last son. This went on for hours, and all I thought was being left behind and I was going to die here on earth. I knew I couldn't protect my son.

A great earthquake began, things were falling, and people were running but they could not escape. People died by the thousands, and the people who wanted to die could not. A man jumped from a building that caught fire, he was about thirty feet up, but when he jumped, he did not die he just broke his limbs, and the cry he gave had me in complete fear. Why weren't these people dying? People began falling on their knees asking for forgiveness, it really was too late. There was a man walking through the smoke laughing saying it's too late. He said you people had chance after chance, and now you call on God out of fear? He laughed, this man was walking around telling people how he could save them and how he could make their lives better. He said that if people would just bow down to him all this terror would stop. People gathered around and begged him to save them.

While people were running and screaming this man had a frightening look on his face I knew he was something evil. He sent all those strange beings away, they listened to him, and the people marveled as he began to make a statue talk. The statue turned his head a full three hundred and sixty degrees I was scared. I thought what demon is this that can make the stone move and talk? People began to say it's God this man made the sky clear up and the sun came out, he told people if they would worship him and him only he would spare their world. People all over rich and small began to give all they had to him. He said he could give them a brand new life, he could make us safe he said those beings were nothing more than aliens, but he could keep them away from earth. He said how our government has lied to us about everything but he is here to bring peace to all nations. He said bow down before your God! We needed a better security system to keep us safe people began to cheer. The man said this was not cheap, but that if we followed him there would be no more wars or poverty we would be just fine. I grabbed my son and hid, I was so afraid. I told him do not be deceived for this is the devil, and he only comes to lie, cheat, and steal. He said those who will not bow down will die right now. I saw hundreds of military trucks coming to get the people who wanted to go, they loaded the people like cattle and off they went, the few hundred that was leaving the man asked them again, who did they want to serve and they said the living Jesus.

Next I saw the man transform into this hideous thirty-foot monster and before a sound could be heard he blew on the people and they turned into dust, like burned ashes, he transformed back into a human. I began to cry, my son was crying, but we followed slowly behind them and we came to a big church looking building. People were going in one door and coming out another, when people came out they looked the same, but they act differently, I also noticed on their forehead was the numbers 666. They were very tiny surrounded by a bar graph and on the outside of their hands was some electronic chip placed in there. With this chip, they could buy food, clothes, cars and all kinds of things, if you did not have this chip you would starve.

In the new testament alone, it mentions the going away or being caught up at least three times, most churches do not preach about hell being a real place, we have been deceived and the only way the devil has been able to fool you is to keep you from praying and repenting. Let me give you a few examples of how we got into this dilemma. First, we have a world that is for homosexuality, and when you live in such a world as this sometimes you are afraid to go against what you know is right, I did not mind this at first I thought live and let live. I wasn't God, how could I say just because you are a homosexual you are going to hell, you can't help who you love right? Wrong. The Bible clearly states this is an abomination to God. There is no other way to say that. But in order to keep the peace most I didn't want to ruffle feathers.

We cheat on our partners, most cheat even on the wedding day. We are fornicators and liars. We are thieves, and we rob God, the world is corrupt. Sexual immorality has taken over, and we find whatever excuse to say he's wrong, and we're right, but the wages of sin is death.

Chapter 4

Worshipping False Idols

The Bible clearly states do not worship idols, yet every day we pray to statues. A statue isn't God, it's not Jesus they cannot hear you, only God can help make your prayers known. We all commit sin, but through the grace we are saved. As I said, the news media wanted to say this was an alien invasion when in reality this was the rapture. Now Satan had people getting a chip in their heads and hands, you say this couldn't happen or wouldn't happen. Well how about these animals they're already being chipped and we all knew it, before this happened there was a high school in California passing out RFID cards to track kids in high school. Before this rapture event took place, it started from the nine eleven events, that Americans wanted to feel safer. Well, if you accept this chip you will be accepting the devil himself and from that there is no return. It is better to lose your life in the Lord than to live and lose your soul forever. We all had warnings, but we ignored them, we heard the Bible tell of wars and rumor of wars but still we ignored the Lord. Here are yet more examples in Pakistan and Iran we have innocent men and women dying by the boatloads. There is an armed conflict in Columbia; in South sedan more than 300,000 have perished. You think that's a coincidence? No, it was the telling of things to come. What is my message, don't get left behind? You have people worshipping Satan at vast levels, but I want to ask you, do you think Satan cares about you?

Satan hates man. And you can't ask the devil for something and not give him something in return. So what will it cost you? Your eternal soul. If you had a chance to see hell, would you want to? I know for the price of fame you may bargain, but after your riches and when your time expired would you be willing to burn in a pit of fire if you knew it was real? Re-think it. I use to like astrology, numerology, but thank God he helped me. I know the devil gives powers, but in the end he loses, you have chosen a loser and you are still willing to go to hell. He uses spells and charms to win people back, and we think that's fine. We cheat, and we believe it's okay. We cheat because we have no respect for God or our partners. We have gone too far, and now we must pay the price. Every world has been destroyed for sex immorality; we have so much sex going on it's a shame. In almost every cartoon, the boy character has something pink along with makeup, every show you have some nudity or cursing. Or it's showing the same sex sleeping together. Everywhere you go people seem to be okay with the high sexual content that is in the world, there are few preachers standing up against it, there have been numerous pastors in the media for homosexuality, and still we will not repent. There was a time I assumed we had more prostitution than any state, then I found out that Japan was and is worse than us. They have legalized prostitution at age thirteen. I mean I know pornography is a billion-dollar industry, but is it worth losing your soul? In the time of Noah, they were eating and drinking, having a good old time. Men were sleeping with men, women with women and animals with humans. What do you think happened? God demolished them, they were foretold but no one believed, you are warned but deceived. Just like the Bible says Jesus

people perish for lack of knowledge. In the days of Solomon and Gomorrah that city was doomed; the people even enticed the angels, even
Lot's wife died as she was disobedient. The Roman Empire was destroyed because of the same thing. Many years before us, the world has done the same crimes, and people have died because of them, but I say we are no better. We are doomed, and I believe by far this is the worst time. Have you bothered to realize that at least six or seven times a day we are on camera, we are being filmed all the time, if you don't think so just look around, not to mention Google records everything you do.

Don't get me wrong, it is said that Jesus hates sin, but loves the sinner. Jesus is constantly waiting for us to change, but we never do, we always think we have tomorrow, but one-day tomorrow may never come and he has sent many people in your life to speak the word. But how many times have you closed your curtains, hid, or pretended to listen when you could care less. So many times we call on Jesus only when we are in trouble. I know because I did it. I called on Jesus when I needed a car, or when I needed a bill paid. I treated him as my personal bank. I should have been on my knees saving my soul, but I wasn't. I am guilty, and that is why I was left behind. I could clearly see my faults, but how would I get out this situation. People who were left began hating God, they said he was unfair, people forgot he gave chance after chance. He gave us a way to escape. But we did not listen. We knew this was going to happen, we were warned. When the collapse of the economy happened, we were warned. The media came on TV. And said we were fine, that's when we should have known we were in trouble.

America is sixteen trillion dollars in debt, how do you expect us to recover from this? We will not. I don't care who is elected, do not be fooled, we are in trouble. When the dollar loses its value, do you think they are going to make an announcement on television? Heck no. You will wake up, go to the bank and try to withdraw twenty dollars, and the teller will tell you insufficient funds!

Oh, this can't happen, well it happened in Argentina, a little more than ten years ago and the only people who had money was the elite people who knew about it and was able to convert their dollars. Common people, average, everyday hard working people like you and I will be left behind. They say that's why so many people are buying silver, and gold. Maybe that's true. But what good will bars of silver and gold do for you if you are left? All that you have will be given to the anti-Christ. You see I too have bought metals, but what I hoped to do with them is eat. In the event all the money was gone, I hope I have something left to trade, I thought I would be gone, but I'm here. You think this could not happen, but you watched your pensions vanish right before your eyes. It's not just America; it's Spain, Greece, Ireland, and E.U. all these states are in trouble. We're all scrambling to stay afloat. There are well over seven billion people in the world, so who do you think will survive? It's the people with the vegetable gardens and the people who own cows, but when the rapture came none of this mattered. I'm just saying how did we get here? Our money says in God we trust, but the world is divided. We say we love God, but our actions clearly say something different. We heard the rumor of wars, but we did not believe. We knew that Russia, Iran and North Korea had weapons of mass destruction, but we did nothing. Can you tell me of another time in history when the world had these weapons to destroy an entire planet? Jesus said the rapture would happen in a twinkling of an eye, do you know how fast that is? Before you could blink, people would be gone. 1corinthians chapter fifteen verse fifty-one and fifty-two tell all about it. This is written in the holy bible, and I believe every word ever written. Revelation twenty-two verse seventeen says whoever desires; *let him take the water of life freely.* This does not mean that everyone will go to heaven, they still must be found in the book of life. See *people are warned that if they add anything to the Bible or take anything away their name will be removed from the book of life according to Revelation twenty-two verse eighteen and nineteen.* You have to ask yourself what do you think you deserve from God? Jesus reward is with him. Are you a liar, a thief, a cheat? Well, I want to tell you no matter what you have done, you can be saved, but when the preacher said that I thought I had time, my time ran out, and I knew I had no time not even to save my boys. Well, as the people were coming out this building with the numbers on them, they were being dropped off at an apartment complex. This place was like a big jail. The people had hundreds of guards, and if they tried to escape, they were shot on contact. The people were in a line the next day marching as far as the eye could see. They were crying, but no one seemed to care.

What I noticed was the women who were strong and beautiful was impregnated by demons and held in a special place. The men and children worked from sun up till sun down, and all praised the anti-Christ. If you did not worship him, you were killed. I saw people only a few hundred who manage to flee, but they left behind children and wives who were subjects to this torture. The people who escaped went undergrounds and Satan gave the orders to find them and kill them. The people could not eat or sell anything without this mark. The oceans had turned to blood; the animals were dying. People did not know what to do. People worked, but didn't get paid. There was no more freedom of speech, there was no more life as we knew it. We were slaves. When the free people ran away, they came up looking for food but all they found was rotten flesh and dead carcasses some died, some got away. The buildings were constantly burning, the nights grew cold, but now only death and diseases covered the earth. We now had a new world order, and this time there was no difference in the classes of people we were all one. Still, I kept thinking this is a dream, I might wake up. I kept saying all the good deeds I'd done, I heard in my spirit you are not saved by good works, good people don't go to heaven, saved people go. Jesus came back for *a holy people.* If we are all sinners, then how are we good in comparison to Jesus? Nope I think not. We don't even come close we are like filthy rags under his feet. Have you ever heard that term keep oil in your lamp? Well, I suggest we all keep the night light burning brightly, as we have no idea when he may come. He said he would come like a thief in the night, if a person knew when a thief would come they would prepare. The reason you will not to know was for you always to be ready. I know for years we heard that he was coming, but he never came, what Jesus did tell you was when you heard certain things the time was at hand. My question is do we not believe? Jesus is the only way to get saved, while I was in the world I forgot that or maybe I just didn't care either way you can't get into heaven unless you believe in your heart that Jesus is the Son of God.

Then you must believe he died for your sins, then you must repent and ask him to come into your heart. Walking a godly life is not easy, it may be the hardest thing you do. Jesus said take up your cross, are you willing to do that? To take up your cross you may have to die for Christ, are you prepared for that, or are you prepared for people to reject you and laugh at you? Are you ready for the insults? Don't get me wrong as many will laugh many will pray with you. Many will bind demons in Jesus name. But know this, the world hated Jesus before you, and since they hated Jesus they will also hate you.

Chapter 5

One God

People say Allah and Jesus are one, but I'll tell you they're not. Allah can mean many things in the Muslim dialect but Jesus is the only way. Now concerning prayer, Jesus mention only one way in Matthew and it starts with the Lord's Prayer. After that make your petitions known to God.

When I was young, I lied, cheated, and sex was like soda. I never knew what flavor I was going to try. If God took my life at that time I would have been in hell, there are too many Christians who doesn't take this seriously. We preach a prosperity prayer, God wants you to be rich and happy, but when God talks about the blessings of tithes he means more than a big house and a fancy car. The Lord will give you wisdom and understanding, love and patience. Which are true blessings if you have never had them. Some people live in hate every day of their lives, just being able to sleep through the night would be a blessing. We need to preach the truth, we need to talk about hell and heaven, people need to be on their knees asking for forgives, daily. When you love Jesus you are a Jesus freak, when you love a singer its normal. Talk about Jesus.

Let me also tell you something you might not know or never heard of, do you know the police have a device in their car that can detect radiation? Yes, this is true. Now what would be the reason for that? Do your investigation and pass it along? What does that tell you, that tells me that people are worried about war.

***

I was looking at people crying after they were hauled to these camps. There was a loud boom the sky got darker than before. Something dropped, I tried to run, but I couldn't. I started to jump on what looked like a hole in the ground, but before I reached the hole I vanished.

***

I saw more people who disappeared, we were high above earth, but in a different body. The body was clear. We were aware of what was going on although we seemed very afraid. I was able to look down and I saw thousands being killed by this big boom, a cloud came down, and I could see hundreds on hundreds following this Lamb who'd been slain. In his right hand was righteousness and the left was death. The graves were open, and all you could see was the demons transforming and coming to the earth, the few who was alive began to scream, and beg God for mercy. Their cries went unanswered. The battle had begun, Jesus came back to take over and cast Satan into the bottomless pit. Satan fought hard and killed many humans. Children turned against parents, parents turned against children. It was an all-out war as Satan promised a new world if people would join him. The war went on for hours, we stayed in the sky, I saw an angel with the face of a lion and the body of a man. He was about thirteen feet, and the light from him was so bright it seemed to create solar flares from the skies. I thought I was in heaven, but then he directed people to walk straight and the people in front of me began falling off what seemed to be a cliff, the cliff was steep, but people realized they were falling into burning fire.

They tried to hold on but they couldn't. When they were holding on something was pulling them down with massive hands, that they couldn't see. The line was long and people were talking in the back, not knowing they were falling into hell. When it came to me the book was open, and I began to cry, my heart was pumping, I asked for a second chance, before I knew it I transported somewhere else. My body was in a room with a big hall and along these halls they had what looked like millions of mailboxes. Inside each of these mailboxes was people's prayers that went up to heaven, but not only was it prayers, it was people's secret sinful desires, I then was moved to a room with a Huge projection T.V.

It was my entire life and all the things I had done. Not only that, I saw my conception, and how I came through and into more sin. I saw the things my mother went through; I began to cry. She was abused just like me. Tears burned my face, I was so afraid. I seemed to be good until the age of six. I began to explore sexuality when I was abused by my family, it went on and showed all my dirty deeds, the things I thought only I knew. I learned that an angel was recording everything I had done. I tried to apologize, but the angel let me know that even after I was baptized I left God.

The angel said, *God kept calling you, you were bringing many to Christ. God never left you*.

I pleaded for a second chance, "I could do better, I promise."

He said, *the judgments were in, my time was up. It is appointed once for man to die after that, the judgement.* Then he took me back to the line, I stood falling off a cliff regretting my life. Regretting yelling at my husband. My sins were addictive and if God can hear me right now I am truly sorry. I felt hot air touching my body as the air grew thick. The fall seemed like an endless pit but I soon came to a stop.

I fell in hell the fire was massive, this place was dark, things and creatures everywhere. The people were not screaming but wailing. There were many actors in hell, many priests. You could see the shapes of people screaming, no one came to help you, God was not with you not in this place. I heard an angel say man is a worm, I thought what does that mean, I thought about psalms and remembered a passage I read in Psalm 22 verse 6 and *after I saw the peoples' bodies burn down to their skeletal form I knew we were nothing more than dust and worms.*

People say hell isn't real, but it's a trick of the devil, he wants you to believe it so you can continue to live recklessly. The devil wants all mankind to die, Satan is mad that angels serve us. Satan feel as though we should serve them since they were created first. I cried and cried, but there was no help for me. I was being thrown around with great ease, and my worst fears tortured me. I remember everything that was going on. Soon I fell on my knees, and said, "God if you can hear me, I now know I'm a sinner, but if you give me a chance I will change, I will preach the word and will live by the word."

Hell was not made for man; Hell is a real literal place where your soul will live forever. Hell isn't harming your body; it's harming something far worse. Your soul.

Chapter 6

What If

Within moments my heart was pumping with fear, I ran into my kids room to see if they were there.

"What are you doing?" Josh asked.

"Did I go somewhere?" I asked him.

He asked, "are you trying to skip this conversation?" I began to cry,

I told my husband, "I'm sorry for being a cheater and first thing tomorrow I would rededicate my life to Christ."

I don't know if this was a vision or a dream but it happened. I was lost, and felt safe coming back. When I came, I decided to write about this. What if it happened tomorrow, what if it happened tonight, would you be ready? Try closing your eyes, now imagine everyone you love vanishing except you, what would you do.

As I said today preaching is watered down, people want you to believe in this prosperity thing and forget that no matter how good you feel sin is unacceptable to God. Everyone sinner will have their part in the lake of fire, just like I did. Towards the end of time, all the preachers will come together for the good of mankind, but I say a lot of religions are different, but don't be fooled. *We all do not worship the living Christ.* And all will not be saved. I know a lot of Christians who go to church every day, sometimes six days a week, but as soon as they leave, they fornicate, curse and go out to get drunk. I 'm not saying people don't repent because every day they do, but repent means to turn away from your sins and not to commit them again.

So what does that mean? Well if you have to change friends, then do it, if you have to change jobs then do it, whatever you need to do just do it? You may have to throw away your computer; if you're addicted to anything it is better to rid yourself of it than to lose your life. For those who feel I'm crazy or I simply have no idea what I'm talking about I will give you scriptures to what I'm saying, then check for yourself. As I said earlier, the Bible mentions the lord's return more than three times. But for the sake of time and reading I will stick to the book of Matthew. In Matthew twenty-four verse twenty-nine it clearly states *after the tribulation, the sun will be darkened, and the moon will not give light, the stars will fall from heaven, from this Jesus will come in a cloud.* Now I know this is a lot of mumble jumble to people, but those who don't believe you will wish for death but will not see death until the coming of Jesus. You can find this in Matthew chapter sixteen verse twenty - eight. What does that mean? It means many who did not believe will then believe, but it will be too late. I like to think of America as one of the greatest places in the world, don't get me wrong, we have many things in our history that's awful. But as a nation we have grown tremendously. I still don't understand people who can look at the sky and tell the weather but cannot discern the end of times, Hypocrites! We are that indeed. We believe people but not God. Matthew chapter sixteen verses three tells this very thing, here is the sign of the times take heed to this warning it begins in Matthew twenty-four with verse five. Many will claim to be Christ, you know this isn't a lie; people have claimed this very thing and had people killed. You need proof here is a list:

Haile Selassie I (1892–1975), the Rastafarian movement that emerged in Jamaica during the 1930s believes he is the Second Coming (although he did not encourage this belief). He embodied this when he became Emperor of Ethiopia in 1930, perceived as confirmation of the return of the Messiah in the prophetic Book of Revelation 5:5 in the New Testament, but is also expected to return a second time to initiate the apocalyptic Day of Judgment. He is also called Jah Ras Tafari, and is often considered to be alive by Rastafari movement members. [7]

George Ernest Roux (1903–1981), called the "Christ of Montfavet" or "Georges-Christ", [8] founder of the Universal Christian Church (now named the Universal Alliance) in France, claimed to be Jesus, then God. He presented himself as a persecuted prophet to carry out the law of love unfulfilled by God's representatives, including Jesus. [9]

Ernest Norman (1904–1971), an American electrical engineer who co-founded the Unarius Academy of Science in 1954, was allegedly Jesus in a past life, and his earthly incarnation was as an archangel named Raphael. [10] He claimed to be the reincarnation of other notable figures, including Confucius, Mona Lisa, Benjamin Franklin, Socrates, and Queen Elizabeth I, and Tsar Peter I the Great. [11]

Krishna Venta Krishna Venta (1911—1958), born Francis Herman Pencovic in San Francisco, founded the WKFL (Wisdom, Knowledge, Faith and Love) Fountain of the World cult in Simi Valley, California in the late 1940s. In 1948, he stated that he was Christ, the new messiah and claimed to have led a convoy of rocket ships to Earth from the extinct planet Neophrates. He died on 10 December 1958 after being suicide bombed by two disgruntled former followers who accused Venta of mishandling cult funds and having been intimate with their wives.

Ahn Sahng-Hong (1918–1985), a South Korean who founded the World Mission Society Church of God in 1964, who consider him the Second Coming of Jesus. The church believes that his wife Zahng Gil-Jah is "God the Mother," who they believe is referred to in the Bible as the New Jerusalem Mother (Galatians 4:26, and that Ahn Sahng-Hong is God the Father [12]

Jim Jones (1931–1978), founder of Peoples Temple, which started off as an offshoot of a mainstream Protestant sect before becoming a personality cult as time went on. He claimed to be the reincarnation of Jesus, Akhenaten, Buddha, Vladimir Lenin, and Father Divine in the 1970s. [15]
Organized a mass murder-suicide at Jonestown, Guyana on 18 November 1978. [16]

Marshall Apple White (1931–1997), an American who posted a famous Usenet message declaring, "I, Jesus—Son of God—acknowledge on this date of September 25/26, 1995: "[17] Apple white, and his Heaven's Gate cult committed mass suicide on March 26, 1997 to rendezvous with what they thought was a spaceship hiding behind the comet Hale-Bopp. [18]

Yahweh Ben Yahweh (1935–2007), born as Holon Mitchell, Jr., A black nationalist and separatist who created the Nation of Yahweh in 1979 in Liberty City, Florida. His selfproclaimed name means "God, Son of God." He could have only been deeming himself to be "son of God", not God, but many of his followers clearly deem him to be God Incarnate. [19] [20] In 1992, he was convicted of conspiracy to commit murder and sentenced to 18 years in prison. [21]

Laszlo Toth (1940–), Hungarian-born Australian who claimed he was Jesus Christ as he vandalized Michelangelo's Pietà with a geologist's hammer in 1972. [22][23]

Wayne Bent (1941–), also known as Michael Travesser of the Lord Our Righteousness Church. He claims; "I am the embodiment of God. I am divinity and humanity combined."[24] He was convicted on 15 December 2008 of one count of criminal sexual contact of a minor and two counts of contributing to the delinquency of a minor in 2008. [25]

Ariffin Mohammed (1943–), also known as "Ayah Pin", the founder of the banned Sky Kingdom in Malaysia in 1975. He claims to have direct contact with the heavens and is believed by his followers to be the incarnation of Jesus, as well as Shiva, and Buddha, and Muhammad. [26]

Mitsuo Matayoshi (1944–), a conservative Japanese politician, who in 1997 established the World Economic Community Party based on his conviction that he is God and Christ, renaming himself Iesu Matayoshi. According to his program, he will do the Last Judgment as Christ, but within the current political system.

José-Luis de Jesus Miranda (1946–), Puerto Rican founder, leader and organizer of Growing in Grace-based in Miami, Florida, who claims that the resurrected Christ "integrated himself within me" in 2007. [29]

Shoko Sahara (1955–) founded the controversial Japanese religious group Aum Shinrikyo in

1984. He declared himself "Christ", Japan's only fully enlightened master and the "Lamb of God". His purported mission was to take upon himself the sins of the world. He outlined a doomsday prophecy, which included a Third World War and described a final conflict culminating in a nuclear "Armageddon", borrowing the term from the Book of Revelation 16:16. [33] Humanity would end, except for the elite few who joined Aum. [33] The group gained international notoriety on 20 March 1995, when it carried out the Sarin gas attack on the Tokyo subway. He has been sentenced to death/ and is awaiting execution.

David Koresh (1959–1993), born Vernon Wayne Howell, was the leader of a Branch Davidian religious sect in Waco, Texas, though never directly claiming to be Jesus himself, proclaimed that he was the final prophet and "the Son of God, the Lamb" in 1983. In 1993, a raid by the U.S. BATF, and the subsequent siege by the FBI ended with Branch Davidian ranch burning to the ground. Koresh, 54 adults, and 21 children were found dead after the fire extinguished itself. [34]

And this was in the twentieth century. Jesus said you would hear of wars and rumor of wars, nations will rise against nations, famines and earthquakes. Now about famine there are many hungry people in the world, in Africa alone people are dying from starvation and aids. And what about the earthquakes, Haiti had one that devastated their entire area, you think this is all a coincidence? All of this is just the beginning of sorrow, and it was foretold more than two thousand years ago. Many will betray one another; many false prophets will rise.

Jesus repeatedly warned His followers saying, _see to it that no one misleads you!_

For the time will come when they will not endure sound doctrine; but wanting to have their ears tickled, they will accumulate for themselves teachers in accordance to their own desires; and will turn away their ears from the truth, and will turn aside to myths.

All this to let you know that although we have seen these things still we don't believe. I am no pastor, I have been a liar, a cheat and many things before, I know people can change, but you can't change by yourself you must incorporate God. The things you have read above, I have found all over the internet and in the King James Bible. I agree with just about all of it, if you want to know why I can't agree with everything it's because I do not know all these men. I don't believe in homosexuality, I just don't. I believe in the Bible, and I believe the Bible was inspired by the word of God. I believe that with God a person can overcome any and everything. Some will read this and take offense, some will see the light, but all will have been warned.

It is said that in Matthew chapter four verse _ten you shall worship the Lord your God and him only you shall serve,_ why is it that we bow down to idols? These are merely stones that cannot hear or see. You need to know you will be tempted, if the devil tempted Jesus then you too will come under attack. You think because you pray and fast and are a Christian that nothing will happen, but be warned you need the whole armor of God. In Matthew chapter four verse one the devil tried to tempt Jesus three times in the last temptation, he even offered him kingdoms, how crazy is that? To offer the king of all kings a kingdom. Jesus did not fall prey to this, he used the Bible against the devil, you must be careful because even the devil knows the word of Christ, and your faith is what the devil fears a faith-based praying Christian. Jesus also talks about the way a pastor should preach, you are to preach the kingdom of heaven is at hand. This is found in Matthew ten verse seven. This isn't to say that pastors shouldn't talk about other things, but above all else they need to let the people know that the time is near constant, repent so that you may be found worthy to be with the father. It's not the will of God that any should perish, but the fact is people are. In Matthew ten verse fifteen it explicitly states *it would be more tolerable for the land of Sodom and Gomorrah in the day of judgment than for that city,* so can you imagine all those do not believe. The pain, wailing, gnashing of teeth. I want to tell the readers *don't fear a person who can kill only the body but fear the one who created you, who can burn body and soul,* Matthew ten verse twenty-eight. *How will you know the anti-Christ, he will be standing in the holy place,* Matthew twenty-four verse fifteen? Can you imagine being judged for everything idle that you have said, well you will. Imagine all the times you have hurt someone feelings, your actions were being recorded. For by your words you are justified, and by your words you are condemned. Most of what I say comes from the Bible this particular passage comes from Matthew chapter twelve verse thirty-six. I hear people say God does not forgive certain sins to my knowledge every sin can be forgiven except the blasphemy of the Holy Spirit.

Matthew twelve verse thirty one and thirty two so with these two verses people should know that they can be forgiven for many things, how good is it to know that God is a loving God who gives multiple chances. Something really unbelievable is the people who worship Buddha and all the other idles, they clean them, some make sacrifices, but when it comes to a God that people can't see. They don't want to believe. Do you remember the time Moses went up to the mountain and saw the people became restless and created their version of God? They danced, laughed and had a merry old time, but what happened after that? Yes, people were destroyed, but before that the people had a chance to choose who'd they would serve. You see, God is a gentleman, he does not force this on you, you see him every day the way the trees move. In the way the ocean never gets higher no matter how much it rains. You can see this in great animals he has created both small and large. The sky is infinity and beyond. Man is trying hard to duplicate what God has created, but they can't. We are cloning, some say we have machines to make thunderstorms. Man seems to be worshiped, and praised. We have forgotten all the things God have done to get him there. Kings are kings because of God. Presidents rule because God had appointed time for them, and the same breath God designates God will take away.

Can anyone tell me what will a man give in exchange for his soul? God doesn't need your money, you can't bribe him, you won't have time to beg, and so then what will you give the Lord for your soul? I hear people saying the end is near, yes this is true, but then I hear people giving a date, that is false. The Bible clearly states no one knows the day or hour in which Jesus is coming back. We still marvel over the gossip. I once was guilty of this, but no longer am I. I say trust what the Bible says. I see on T.V that people who are preparing for the end times, when the end happens the anti-Christ will find you, you will suffer, small and great will receive those numbers it has already been foretold. I struggle not to laugh when I see such shows. I know people take this seriously, but if you are saved and you believe, then you have no worries about what will happen because you know you won't be here. I see people with stocked up food, I think that's great, but I must remind you that the Lord is in control, not man. Clearly, in Matthew, Jesus talks about the rapture and how the Jesus lovers will be taken and the others left behind. Many will be saved, but not the seven billion in the world. The question you want to ask yourself is are you one of the chosen one? The angels will gather all the good because of them our days in the tribulation will be shortened. Towards the end there is much speculation about Jesus having a perfect world. I believe when Jesus rid the world of all the bad the world will be as he said. When I read Matthew thirteen verse thirtyseven I was confused, I knew the passage had something to do with the devil and the world, but then the more I read more I realized the field is the word, the good seed are the sons of the kingdom. The tares are the one from Satan. The enemy who sowed them is the devil, and the harvest is the end of age. The reapers are the angels the tares will be gathered and burned in the fire, and this will be the end of age. Even in Matthew chapter thirteen verse forty-two it talks about casting people into the furnace of fire, wailing, and gnashing of teeth again in verse forty-nine wailing, and gnashing of the teeth. God has foretold hell and the end of this world as we know it. Still, we don't believe. With all I have been told even I have backslidden, you have to praise God alone for his mercy he has shown humankind.

Chapter 7

The Greatest Is Love

Here's a story for young girls who should say no. As women you should love yourself enough to say no when we don't want sex. Most men won't say 'let's wait,' as a matter of fact, all the good looking guys want sex and if you didn't give it up some fast girl will. Most girls want popularity they just don't know the cost. I began having sex, and continued until I'd become pregnant. Imagine the shock when a girl gets pregnant, most girls think they have sex without consequences. We think pregnancy could never happen to us, we have sex, but never think about a baby. Here I am a young mother with a child. We're just children ourselves. We secretly want an abortion, but have no way to pay for it. My is life ruined? Will I be on welfare like the three generations in my family? What will I do? Will my boyfriend help me? Will we be a family?

I have the child, and was alone, my family was there but the boy who loved me every day, never showed up. He loved me as long as my legs were opened. He loved me as long as I stayed out all night. He loved me as long as I dressed like a whore, but the moment I became his baby mama he didn't know us. He didn't know his child, we fought all the time from the moment became I had a baby. I needed money for our child, I needed help and all he said was go home and find someone else. It's funny now when I met this boy I never asked 'can you read?' I never asked 'do you have a job.' You never asked 'what are your goals?' Funny how now after the birth you wanted to know all these things. He treated you like dirt, you must take full responsibility for this.

The Bible says no fornication; I did not heed those words. If I had listened we would not have been in this mess, I would've done things the right way, like get married first, but so many men want sex. So much on television makes you think about sex, all my friends were having sex at the time.

After we had our child I said this would never happen again, well two years past, and here I go again with a different man, this guy was college educated, he had a nice body. I thought this made for a great recipe, what I didn't know was this man was over protective. Still living with his mother, while having a well-paid career. Still I gave him the benefit of the doubt.

Soon after that fool I met another young man who had the best sex one could ask for, he had no job, no car and sex soon got old, at the time all we cared about was our needs. I knew one thing no man was going to live with us, I already had one child and I was working so we felt independent.

As a woman we sometime grow up and think in order to be loved that we need a man, this is not so. The greatest love in the world was when Jesus died on that cross for you. He loved you so much that he was willing to carry your sins so you would have a second chance at life. There is no greater love than a father who will die for his children.

We believe men all the time when they we are beautiful, but looks fade. Growing up in homes parents should tell their daughters more often how beautiful and wonderful they are, but if they don't, then god thinks your priceless! Stand on this truth and be transformed…

Chapter 8

Thank You!

I woke up at night and sat on my porch talking to the sky, hoping God was listening, I can't forget this it feels like yesterday. I asked God to take me out of the ghetto and let me meet a man who would love my children and I, it happened. It took three years, since the day ten years have passed, I have never been back. I know God hears, and I know he has a plan. Sometimes I don't like it, sometimes I cry, sometimes I ignore it and when I do the results are devastating. Sound bad, but it has been a blessing. I use to cry, but now I shout for joy. Through God, I am an author and my husband truly loves me. I want you to know who the person is writing this book, I came from a humble beginning I slip, and I fall but his grace holds me.

Can you imagine what we would do if Christ had not died on that sweet cross? There had to be blood shed for sinners like us to get an entrance into heaven. God is just that holy. In the old times people made animal sacrifices for sins that were committed, I don't know about you, but I can't even chop off a dead chicken head let alone a live goat. So I thank God. He died for me knowing I was still a sinner.

If you have another God besides the almighty tell me why? What miracles do you believe they perform, and if you died right now can the blood of your god get you into heaven? I know many people who have different religions other than

Christianity and everyone thinks theirs is the right one. But the bible, the Holy Bible has been dissected over and over again and has been proven to have accurate accounts of Jesus Christ. This is not to say that prophets have not existed somewhere else because they have, but Jesus is Jesus, and there is no duplication of him, his birth was foretold seven hundred years before his birth. Think about that, look around you non-believers, see the proof in front of your face. Maybe the trees are too tall? My life and all the things I have been through I know if it weren't for God I would've fainted. There were times that I didn't want to follow him, I wanted to give up, my lights were out, my fridge was empty, and I felt like God could zap some money my way. I lived in this world, and all my lusts came first. I wanted that car, that man, this jewelry. Never knowing that I could have died and been lost. The Bible is clear on a few things let me tell you what that is. Hell, Heaven, and Jesus. Yep, hell is a literal, burning, suffering, painful place that no one wants to go, so if you are a sinner and all of us are, I urge you to repent and make repenting something you do daily. I just wanted to tell God Thank you, for all he has done for me….

Chapter 9

His Holy Place

I hear people say they would rather be in hell rather than earth. Who wants to burn continually? Who? But one thing for sure I'm not going to ask God to let me burn. No way, I want the peace that God offers. I want to live in the golden mansion, I want to see the jewel paved streets. I want to hear this fantastic singing of the angels. Sometimes when I think of heaven, I begin to cry, it's a place where I can be a safe child in my father home. I never dreamt about how wonderful it would be in hell, burning, screaming, and wishing I had a second chance at life. I don't care who's down there, I don't want to be with them.

I pray for the lost every night, and I hope that my family isn't down there, but you never know. In every family you have sinners, even I was a true sinner at a time. The thought of burning is what keeps me repenting, almost every day I get mad at something, but I never stay mad more than sixty seconds, I want to forgive, I try to forgive because I want God to forgive me. People who have died say that they have seen heaven well, I just open the Bible to revelation and read.

Imagine living in a gold mansion, can you believe that, even if you won the lottery here, would you be in a gold mansion, I envision flowers that smell like jolly ranchers, and a lake so clear that I can see my reflection as if looking in a mirror. I think I will be able to have friends who will like me for me not for what I have. Trees that never lose its color, and food for all.

Here on earth people starve, sometimes children die, sadness is all around, too many never help. When I think of heaven, I think of a place that Jesus has stored up for believers. A place where sickness will be no more, a place we can see our loved ones, a place we can be free of all problems. I dreamt of a place like this. I have looked to the clouds quite often and wonder if God sees me, but after this dream not only can he see me, but he is recording all my actions and yours too. The only thing on my mind is, if this is a dream then you have nothing to worry about, when it's your time to die you can rest assured you will turn to dirt and be no more, but if I'm right and you know you are living a life of sin then your life as you know it will end. Are you willing to pay the ultimate price? Are you willing to burn in an unnatural fire, or willing to be tortured? If not, then I plead with you to repent, ask for forgiveness and truly change your life. It's not the Lord will that you should perish.

Chapter 10

God Loves You If No One Else Does

There are times when we feel unloved, I get it. I can't say I really had love, I just didn't, what I had was a house and no home. I thought my life was good, but as I grew older I had many missing links and no one was there to help me. This isn't to say that it's anyone's fault because right now I know it's not. Don't blame my mother for not raising me. As I said earlier, because truth is she did the best she could with what she had. Her choices were hers and the life she is living belongs to her. She has no one to answer but God, the truth is if my mother never did any of the things I thought she did I would not be a write this book. Some of my greatest pain has turned into ink for others to read. People say what doesn't kill you makes you stronger, well there is some truth to that, God also says he will give you no more than you could bare. At the time when any of us is going through trials we always think it's too much, but most times we come through and can always say God made a way, when all doors appeared closed. There was a time when I thought it was better to die than to live, I now know that Satan wanted me to do that, my life was never my own to take, I am here renting this body God gave to me and when my time comes I will leave this body. I only hope that I can help people see that God has a plan for their life. And I'm not saying that everyone plans to be rich, that may not be in the cards for you. What you hear from preachers, but maybe your job is to help a lost soul. Maybe it's to put a smile on a child face who feels unappreciated. When you're in your darkest hour, and you feel that hope is gone reach your arms out and although you can't see him, Jesus is there waiting to hug you and tell you things will get better. I work with Atheist and all kinds of people, some who never claim to have believed in God, but if you ever really just read the bible and do some real investigations you will begin to ask yourself how you could not believe in him. I don't argue with God I don't have to. Its your choice to believe in God, my job is to share him with the world, I leave everything else up to God, he's pretty big and I have the faith that he could handle it.

There were times in my life where my mouth got me into trouble, I thought having a big mouth was cool. I thought if I had a smart mouth, I would be popular and get me some attention, well I got attention just not the kind I wanted. There was a time I was in school, I was failing everything, not because I couldn't pass I was just interested in boys, so I thought being cool was better than school. I had this teacher who I talked bad about all the time to all the kids, I was pretty bad. I hated him or so I thought but what I really had was selfhatered. Well, one day I guess the kids went back and told him everything I said, he called me out of class to question me about what some kids said. Well of course, my mouth literaly did all the talking and he hit me square in the face. The teacher and I began to rumble down the halls, inside I was scared to death. I wanted my mother to save me, I wanted my father to do something. Well, no father ever came, soon my mother came once the teacher got off of me by another teacher pulling us apart. Instead of suing the school my mother allowed this private school to bump my grades up and off I went to ninth grade. Now at the time I wasn't mad, I had a chance to start over and that's what I did.

It wasn't till years later with my mother that this conversation would come up, when my son was harmed and I called her for help. She told me, "if I hadn't been a working mother this would never happen," for a split second her words rang truth in my ears, my tears burned my cheeks.

I quickly had a comeback I yelled at her, "well what kind of mother were you, to let a teacher jump on your child and do nothing about it?" My blood boiled with both, fear and anger.

My mother responded, "you deserved it, and why are you calling me. I hate you!" To this day I have never forgotten that conversation, all I could do was to hang up. I cursed the day she was born at that time, then I hugged my child soon after I began going back to church here. I knew from that occasion that I needed God because I secretly hated my mother, and I didn't want to feel that way, I wanted to love her despite all I thought she had done, despite whatever I did to her, it wasn't easy. It's hard to love a person when you're so much like them, when you hate their ways but you realize you act just like them. As I said my mother was beautiful, and maybe that was the problem, beauty is just that and in the long run beauty fades then what's left? I have so many people that I talk to who felt unloved, because some were overweight, because some were dark. Mines started at home, my mother started at home.Therapy was needed for her and me, I finally got the help and set my soul free, but what I want to tell my readers, you can't make a person love you, can't buy a person's love, they either want to give it freely or they don't, you, can't force yourself upon another. You have to give pain up, don't hold on to the past and hurt that come along with the pain. Pain is a part of life we have to be willing to take, have enough faith that change comes in the morning. Your life will change, this is a book about you trusting in God, he will change your life, love is something we take for granted every day. We abuse the love of people dear to us. We hurt the ones we love and then we expect understanding. God gave many commandments, but out of all the commandments, love was the greatest! Keep your pride!

Grace

There was a time that I had no idea what the grace of Jesus was or even what it meant, I am sure that I am not by myself. Once you come to know God you realize how grateful you are. The world does not deserve him, but thank God that we are saved, because what if that was not the case?

There were times in my life when I wanted to give up as I stated before suicide seemed like the best option, in reality my problems never went away but the burden became much lighter. The other day I went to church like usual, but this Sunday was a bit unusual, when the pastor began to speak he started talking about tithing and how some pastors preach God will give you more in monetary values. I was one of those people who went to church, heard the word and gave all I had, the reality was I was still hungry and my bills still needed to be paid, I gave expecting more money back because my pastors taught that, I never appreciated the things I've received from God, I treated God like a Genie. I wanted him to grant all my requests. I gave up those thoughts when one day I was pregnant with my son. I had no family this was the only year after my little brother had been killed. I had no numbers in which to call and pride got the best of me. Well, one day my husband had gone shopping and three weeks later he was going to see his mother for the holidays.

While pregnant I had a few other boys to raise, and the boys would sneak into the kitchen at all times of the night to eat food. Now I had no idea this was happening, I figured we had enough food for at least three weeks until he came back. We had no home phone, no cell phone I was kind of isolated. At the time it didn't bother me until the fatal day that I realized we had nothing to eat, I remember watching T.V. and seeing all these pastors saying call in for prayer. I would use the neighbor's phone, and ask them to send me money for food which they could not. I ask for ten dollars on these hotlines, they said if I left my number they would get back to me, well that never happened. I was down to one box of cornbread and I baked that for all four kids with me telling the oldest two not to eat it, it *had* to last for a week. Well as soon as we went to sleep, the kids ate it all up from me and the youngest two. I began to cry, the kids had no idea what they had done, but they were about to find out. On the day that the kids ate the bread a few hours later they were hungry. I told the oldest ones to begin looking for pennies around the house, so we could buy noodles. My middle son had the saddest look on his face and I will never forget it, but with joy he helped me look for pennies. My youngest two never cried, they were the best, and my oldest son was so mad that every time I looked at him I wanted to spank him. When I looked back on it I was the adult not them. What have I done, why was I in this situation? We found enough pennies to eat for three nights and I had to hide the noodles I bought. I was in fear that my kids would eat it all and we would die a slow death. I had not eaten nothing for about a week my strength was gone, and it was now Christmas. I never spoke to my husband and he didn't write, he couldn't call and I was only two hours away, and he didn't come by. I was on my own. I was scared and where in the hell was this damn preacher at. Who said if I *tithed*, God would give me all that I asked for?

Well that never happened, at the end of the first week I took a hot bath and cried in the water. I asked God, *where are you*, I begged him to help but received no reply. I rubbed my stomach and inside I could feel the baby moving. I begged God not to let my child die. I held on believing that there must be a way out, I rubbed my stomach with each passing day knowing that it has to get better. I thought God hated me, I thought all the things I had done had finally caught up with me. I ran away from my past with the hopes of starting a new life, and now I was suffering. I was skin and bones I had shaved off my hair and the only weight I seemed to have was this kid in my belly. I never felt sorry for myself just for my kids as they didn't ask for this, I brought them to this and again I was mad at the preachers. I thought they were supposed to help me but they *did not!* The next day I went to the mailbox, and mail was there, by then we had eaten all the noodles and I thought how was I going to feed my kids. All I saw was bills and more bills. Now about this time, I began to hate my husband, I thought how could I marry such a man, I tried to put these hateful thoughts out my mind and look at the mail, as I looked at the letter I saw one from a famous television ministry and opened the letter. It had one dollar in it, I fell to my knees to thank God and I thanked him for that one dollar. Because that was just enough to buy more food for these kids. Now I could not make this up, this happened. Soon after that I began praying to God for him to help me, I was telling him how I would change and give my life to him and my kids, if only he would make a way out.

Well, not even three days later the food was gone and I was driving around looking for a job while pregnant. I had no luck on the way back home my son notices a person walking with bread.

He said, "hey mom, I think they're giving out free bread." So we would pull over and ask the stranger where was the free food and he told us it was up the street, I drove there and saw a line of people getting bread, I drove home and told the boys to go and get some bread, they did. But when they came back they had all kinds of pies, jelly rolls and donuts it was amazing. I was truly grateful to God, but the tears began to roll, and they didn't stop. I couldn't believe that God in all his mercy and grace was still watching over me. The bread store was there for three days on the fourth day my kids went there and the store had vanished as if it was never there. When my kids went to knock on the owner's door they had no idea what my kids was talking about. I assumed they were lying, so I drove around there, *to my surprise* there were no signs and no bread like before. I came home in shock, I still thanked God for the miracle and believed he would help me, on that day my kids were on their last jelly roll, but I was so grateful I didn't know what to do, when the mail came I expected bills, but what was in the mailbox was a check for three thousand dollars.

Money that was owed that was delayed was right on time, so when I think about his grace I know that *truly* Jesus loves me. Now how does this tie into the other preachers well while at church I had to agree with what the pastor had said God wants you rich but not just with money, sometimes he wants to build your character, sometimes he gives you a loving family and when you feel you don't have that loving family maybe it's your test for you to have more patience, love and understanding. When we give it, should be from the heart, and we should want to give knowing our father already know what we have need of. To put your faith in something you can't see is not that hard when you put your faith in things you can see, and they let you down all the time. Trust only in God, unlike man, he is not a liar, what he says must come to pass.

In Matthew ten verse fifteen it clearly states it would be more tolerable for the land of Sodom and Gomorrah in the day of judgment than for that city, so can you imagine that all you who do not believe, the pain the wailing the gnashing of teeth. I want to tell the readers of this book do not fear a person who can kill the body, but fear the one who created you who can burn body and soul Matthew ten verse twenty-eight. How will you know the anti-Christ, he will be standing in the holy place Matthew twenty-four verse fifteen? Can you imagine being judged for everything idle that you have said, well you will. You will. Imagine all the times you have hurt someone's feelings, or how many times you have laughed at it while someone may have been funny to you, your actions were being recorded. For by your words you are justified, and by your words you are condemned. Keep in mind most of what I say comes from the Bible this particular passage comes from Matthew chapter twelve verse thirty-six. I hear people say that God does not forgive certain sins to my knowledge every sin can be forgiven except the blasphemy of the Holy Spirit. Matthew twelve verse thirty-one and thirty-two, so with these two verses people should know that they can be forgiven. How good is it to know that God is a loving God who gives multiple chances? He forgives nations, and all their idols, they clean them some make sacrifices to them, but when it comes to a God that people cannot see they do not want to believe. Do you remember the time Moses went up to the mountain and the people became restless and created their version of God? They danced, they laughed and had a merry old time, but what happened after that? Yes, people were destroyed, but before that happened, people had a chance to choose who they would serve. You see, God is a gentleman. He does not force this on you; you can see him every day in the way the trees move, in the way the ocean never gets higher no matter how much it rains. You can see this in the great animals he has created both small and large. The sky is infinity and beyond. Man is trying hard to duplicate what God has created, but they cannot. We are cloning; some say we have machines to make thunderstorms. Man seems as if he wants to be worshiped, and praised the man has forgotten all the things that God has done to get him there. Kings are kings because of God; president's rule because God had an appointed time for them, and at the same breath God designates God will take it away. Can anyone tell me what will a man give in exchange for his soul? God does not need your money, you cannot bribe him, and you will not have time to beg, so then what will you give the master for your soul? I hear people saying the end is near, yes, this is true, but then I hear people giving a date, this is false. The Bible clearly states no one knows the day or hour in which Jesus is coming back. We still marvel over the gossip. I too am guilty of this, but no longer. I say trust what the Bible says. I see on T.V that we have the people who are preparing for the end times, but I say to you that when the end comes the anti-Christ will find you, you will suffer, small and great will receive those numbers it has already been foretold. I struggle not to laugh when I see such shows as I know people take this seriously, but if you are saved and you believe, then you have no worries about what will happen to you because you know you will not be here. I see people with stocked up food, well, I think that's great, but I must remind you that the Lord is in control, not man. Clearly, in Matthew, Jesus talks about the rapture and how one will be taken and the other left. Many will be saved, but not the seven billion in the world, the question you want to ask yourself if you are one of the elect. The angels will gather all the elect and because of them our days in the tribulation will be shortened. Towards the end there is much speculation about Jesus having a perfect world; well, I believe when Jesus rid the world of all the bad the world will be as he said. When I read Matthew thirteen verse thirty-seven I was confused, I knew something was of the devil, but then I read more and realized the field is the word the good seed are the sons of the kingdom, but the tares are the one from Satan. The enemy who sowed them is the devil, the harvest is the end of age. And the reapers are the angels the tares will be gathered and burned in the fire, and this will be the end of age. Even in Matthew chapter thirteen verse forty-two it talks about casting people in the furnace of fire, wailing and gnashing of teeth again in verse forty-nine wailing and gnashing of the teeth. God has foretold hell and the end of this world as we know it. But still we do not believe. Like most of my life was sin, I wanted popularity I just didn't know at what cost. When I began to have sex, I continued until I became pregnant, imagine my shock when I was pregnant, you see I thought that could never happen to me, I knew I was having sex but I never thought about a baby. So here I was a young mother with a child. I wanted an abortion as a matter of fact, I begged for one, but my mother said no. I had my son, and I was by myself, my family was there but the boy who said he loved me every day, never showed up. He loved me as long as my legs was opened, he loved me as long as I stayed out all night, he loved me as long as I dressed like a whore, but the moment I became his baby mama he didn't know me. We fought all the time from that moment on, my needing money for my child, me needing help and him saying go home find someone else. It's funny how when I met this boy I never said can you read, I never asked do you have a job? I never said what are your goals? Funny how now after the birth of my son I wanted to know all these things. He treated me like dirt, but at some point I had to blame myself. You see the bible says no fornication, but I did not heed those words. If I would have listened to God, I would not have been in this mess, first I would have done things the right way, like getting married first, but so many men want sex... I had no idea how much I did not love myself... After I had my son I said thaw would never happen to me again, well more than six years past, and here I was again with a different man, this guy was college educated, he had a nice body and he loved his mother. I thought this made for a great recipe, what I did not know was this man was over protective, still living with his mother all while having a well-paid career. I still gave him the benefit of the doubt. We dated, and it landed me into a brief marriage that we both regretted. You see, before I got reborn, I was the type of person that when you made me mad I had to get revenge. And I did just that while I was with this man I found out it, he was cheating and could drink a wino in the gutter. We soon parted thank God for that. You sometimes have blessings in your life, and you have no idea they are from God. Soon after that fool I met another young man who had the best sex one could ask for, but he had no job and no car, and those were important points, but at the time all I cared about was my needs, I knew one thing for sure no man was going to live with me, you see I already had one child, and I was working so I felt independent, but in the wee hours of the night I felt something missing, I needed to know why I was here and what was my assignment, seems like the whole world is looking for the same thing. Sometimes I woke up at night and sat on my porch talking to the sky, hoping God was listening, you see I can't forget this because it feels like yesterday, I asked God to take me out the ghetto and let me meet a man who would love me and my children, and it happened. It took three years, but we left ten years have passed, and I have never been back. I know God hears, and I know he has a plan; sometimes I don't like it, sometimes I cry sometimes I ignore it and when I do the results are devastating. You see my stories are too numerous to tell, but what I will say is somewhere down the road I ended up having five children, and only one father remains and that is my Husband. Sounds bad, but it has been a blessing. I use to cry, but God has turned my tears into joy. Life has not always been easy, and I tell you it will not be easy for you, but with God all things are possible.

The Word became Flesh

What does that mean? Many times while in church and listening to the pastor, I thought the word became flesh, but if you think about it Jesus came here in the flesh to save you. He was willing to leave all the glory and riches to save you. Many times we know that something greater than us do exist, and we know this is Jesus, but we think in our heart that we will change when we get ready on our time, we always think I have time to do this one last thing, well I want to tell you a story of a young girl who waited too late. There was a young girl by the name of Shavon, and she was dating this young man named Stan. When they met, she thought it was love, at first sight, he was a tall, dark man with a muscular build and a smile that won her heart. They met in a welfare office, both were with other people who were applying for aid, Shavon's friend tried to warn her of the dangers of this guy but Shavon did not listen. About three months had gone by before he started beating her, there were nights that her hair was pulled out, and she was left bloody, Shavon never told anybody, mostly out of fear. Stan's family knew he was abusing her, but they were fine with it, most of Stan's family was abused. Shaven was very afraid of him, but that did not stop them from getting married. Night after night Stan tried to get Shavon pregnant, well one night while Shavon was going to work Stan poured juice all over her, he said she was dressed too nice to be going to work, Shavon just cried. Shavon had one friend to call Tamika, now Tamika was a good friend she told Shavon to come to her house, but Shavon was afraid what Stan would do to her family, one night Stan got so drunk and beat Shavon nearly to death, after beating her he raped her, the rape last for about three hours. There was nothing Shavon could do, but allow it to happen. Tears burned as she wondered where God was, but through all of this she was not dead, she thought God had abandoned her, she was alone. One night she called her grandmother for help, she told her grandmother about all the abuse, and that she finally wanted to leave, her grandmother told her to please come. One night after he had beaten her Shavon walked over fifteen miles to get to her grandmother's house. Her nails were broken, her hair was pulled out and her face swollen, when she knocked on the door her grandmother began to cry she told Shavon what had happened to you. Shaven grabbed her granny who then could barely walk and began to cry. She went to the shower and scrubbed the blood off, she tried to scrub the pain and hurt away but could not remove the pain. The water felt as good as the sore broken body. After drying off Shavon went to talk to her grandmother, she said she was sorry for, not listening; she apologized for turning her back on God. She told her grandmother, she was scared and said she had married a crazy man who wanted to beat her. Shavon began to cry and cry; she said how she had ruined her life. She told her grandmother about the long walk and told her she didn't know what gave her the strength to walk for so long. Her grandmother said God has something for you to do and until you do it you will not die, Shavon cried even more she told her grandmother, I am a sinner and God has turned a deaf ear to me. The grandmother told Shavon to lay down and rest while Shavon was sleeping her grandmother was looking at all the bruises that was on her body and she began to cry silently as she knew she was too old to help her granddaughter. So she got on her knees and said, Lord, please help my child, it was about noon the next day when they heard a knock at the door the grandmother went to the door and it was Shavon husband, Stan, in an instance Shavon was terrified she said Granny, please do not let him in, but he persuaded her granny that he only wanted to talk and nothing more, The grandmother lets him in it was almost if Satan he jumped in the grandmother, but I tell you when God has a plan no one and nothing can deter that not even the devil. When the grandmother opened the door, she went back to her room, and Stan grabbed Shavon and punched her square in the face, almost breaking her nose. Shavon got up and began fighting this six foot three amazon man. Shavon was scared for her life, he was too big to fight and how would she win is what Shavon thought, within seconds the grandmother heard the rumbling and came to the living room, but it was too late, they were fighting, the grandmother called other family members hoping this would stop them from fighting, it was in Stan eyes to kill her, since she fought back he needed to teach her a lesson, Stan believed women was to know their place and they needed to do what their husband said. Stan beat her and beat her until she grabbed a knife from the kitchen, the fight stopped for a minute, just enough time for her to say please leave, in a moment Stan had a chance to leave but he did not. He said I will make you eat this knife. He charged Shavon and the fight continued, hit after hit, Shavon wondered why her grandmother did not call the police clearly someone was going to die, but who soul was ready for death? Shavon was scared and did not want this fight, it was either him or her. Within seconds they were fighting over the knife, the knife went in but Stan pulled out and tried to stab Shavon, blood was everywhere, Shavon was screaming, Stan finally fell down Shavon called the police with the hopes of saving this man who seconds earlier tried to kill her, after fighting for her life she was now fighting to save his life. The dispatcher said put a towel on the wound apply pressure, she did until the ambulance came keeping him alive as long as possible, Stan later died at the hospital, this blow left Shavon in a daze and soon she was arrested for murder one. Through all this she wondered where was God, God knew she did not want to kill this man, why didn't he save her, Shavon didn't know then that all this would be a blessing to the Lord and her life would start changing.

Shavon went to jail for thirty days and was released she went to court for about a year and all charges was dropped, they were not dropped because Shavon was special, they were dropped because God never left, while in jail Shavon told me she read Psalm 35 three times a day she told me she had that scripture memorized. Jail was nothing she liked, but she said while she was there she met women who still prayed to God and still read their Bibles every night. She learned a Christian hymn that she still sings to this day that she has since then taught her children. Jail was not in her path to hurt her, but in her path as a stepping stone for her to be greater than what she was.

I often tell people that God is wonderful, I am reminded of how Mandela, although he was imprisoned in terrible conditions God raised him to a life of prosperity. Sometimes in our darkest moment is when the plan has come together, you just can't see it. I often wonder why we give up, is our physical bodies that weak? Well Shavon was weak, she did not pray every night, she did not give freely, and after this ordeal she gave her life to God. Shavon was released from jail there was no welcome party not even her mother there was a family friend who came, I tell you this story to say Jesus came in the flesh and because of this you are blessed, because he laid down his life you are blessed noticed I said laid down his life because no one took his life from him, he truly gave it freely with telling his disciples that the day was soon to come when he could not be with them. I wish life was easy, but like

Shavon found out based on the decisions we make life is up to us. And just because you make bad decisions does not mean your life will not be great. It is when you are broken when you can see god's greatest masterpiece. It's when you are down and out that the Lord steps in and often you don't need to ask, God knows what you need before you ask.

How great is our God? He is awesome his love just makes me cry. For more than thirty years' people had Jesus, they had the teachings of our Lord and savior. The problem with us we need to be clean in order to have God, we cannot be dirty. God has the vision for you; he has the miracle you need but are you really ready for it. God has given each of us a dream, but are you willing to accept it? God has given us dominion over the earth. How wonderful is that. Man has tamed much from the lion of the jungle to the killer whales in the ocean? Please accept what God has to offer often we look to the world for what we need, and because God does not work on our time we do not want to wait on him. We are supposed to honor Mary, his mother, but we are to worship Jesus Christ! That is the name above all names. I thank God that through Mary my savior was born, but that is the only God of the earth. There is only one God that can save you and that's Jesus Christ. So when I say to you the word became flesh, thank God it did for people like Shavon, like me so that we all have a second chance at life, if Stan knew that on that day his soul would be required of him do you think he would have changed? My answer to you is no because he liked the way he lived, and he believed that he had time. He made people's life hell on earth every day. When Jesus died, Satan jumped for joy as he thought Jesus was finished, but Jesus got up and went to hell and took the keys and three days later his body, not his spirit rose up. Jesus took the keys from Satan's house and knowing this you can be free from any addiction and any despair that you are going through. When Jesus spirit is over you all will know, by the way, live. When Jesus comes to help, you don't need anybody.

Glory to God for the coming of his son. Guard your heart, watch what you say watch what you do. Your body is a temple. First Cor. Chapter six. What does that mean? Take care of your body and do not corrupt it. People think Jesus spirit was lifted, but it was his body and Jesus's bought your body by his blood, by his stripes you are healed, so if you have cancer or any disease then claim it and know by his stripes you are healed. And please remember that without him you can do nothing but with him all things are possible.

I have been asked over and again why you believe in something you cannot see. Is it easier to have faith in gold or silver just because you can see it? I went to church it was one day before Christmas; I questioned why we really celebrate? Long before Jesus was born the pagans were already giving gifts, decorating trees and having huge feasts in honor of the sun god. Around Dec 25 they realized the days were getting longer and the sun God was blessing them. So they gave gifts to him, lit bonfires, As I went out shopping like most people I was caught in the hustle and bustle of the new year, everyone buying toys and all the latest gadgets to please one another, I saw trees of all colors and tinsel and all the fixings to make this Christmas bright, what I didn't see was a lot of Christmas about Jesus. I asked the manager where was the Christian section to buy gifts for Christmas. I asked for a cross and emblems that were Christian, but he quietly told me they did not sale those items at his store I asked why? he said it was so he did not offend the different type of people.

How we don't want to offend the atheist or any nonbeliever, I thought this was a country built on the Word of God, our money even says in God we trust. But we deny prayer and anyone who speaks against homosexuality, anger, lust, and fornication is considered strange, people say that when you talk about Jesus too much, you are a Jesus freak, but when you agree with the world the world loves you, you cannot follow God and the world you must make a choice, and the choice is yours. You must know that Jesus is the only way. There is no book but the Bible in which the word is real and alive Now, whether you believe in Christ or not, the question is if he is the Messiah, then if you believe he is, then celebrate his life and death because in his death you have life.

Rapture in 1 Thessalonians 4, 1 Corinthians 15:

There is no debate that 1 Thessalonians 4 and 1 Corinthian 15 teach on the rapture. Both chapters also teach the resurrection and of the trumpet blast. Neither chapter mentions anything about having to endure the tribulation before the rapture comes. There is no debate that Revelation 19 and Zechariah 14 teach about the physical return of the Lord Jesus Christ in power after the tribulation. Neither of those chapters speaks of the rapture nor of a resurrection, nor of a trumpet blast.

1 Thessalonians 4:15 for this we say unto you by the word of the Lord, that we which are alive and remain unto the coming of the Lord shall not prevent them which are asleep.

1 Thess 4:16 For the Lord himself shall descend from heaven with a shout, with the voice of the archangel, and with the trump of God: and the dead in Christ shall rise first:

1 Thess 4:17 then we which are alive and remain shall be *caught up* together with them in the clouds, to meet the Lord in the air: and so shall we ever be with the Lord. 1 Thess 4:18 Therefore comfort one another with these words.

1 Thess 1:10 and to wait for his Son from heaven, whom he raised from the dead, even Jesus, which *delivered us from the wrath to come.*

1 Thess 2:19 for what is our hope, or joy, or crown of rejoicing? Are not even ye *in the presence of our Lord Jesus Christ at his coming*?

1 Thess 5:9 For *God hath not appointed us to wrath,* but to obtain salvation by our Lord Jesus Christ,

1 Thess 5:23 and the very God of peace sanctify you wholly and I pray God your whole spirit and soul and *body be preserved blameless unto the coming* of our Lord Jesus Christ.

1Cor 15:51 Behold, I show you a mystery; we shall, not all sleep, but we shall all be changed, 1Cor 15:52 in a moment, in the twinkling of an eye, at the last trump: for the trumpet shall sound, and *the dead shall be raised incorruptible, and we shall be changed.* 1Cor 15:53 for this corruptible must put on incorruption, and this mortal must put on immortality.

1Cor 15:54 So when this corruptible shall have put on incorruption, and this mortal shall have put on immortality, then shall be brought to pass the saying that is written, Death is swallowed up in victory.

1Cor 15:55 O death, where is thy sting? O grave, where is thy victory?

Luke 21:36 Watch ye therefore, and *always pray, that ye may be accounted worthy to escape all these things that shall come to pass* and to stand before the Son of man.

The Seven Churches; One is promised an Escape through the "open door" from the Great Tribulation

To Thyatira:

Rev 2:22 Behold, I will *cast her* into a bed, and them that commit adultery with her *into great tribulation,* except they repent of their deeds.

To Philadelphia:

Rev 3:8 I know thy works: behold, I have set before thee an *open door,* and no man can shut it: for thou hast a little strength, and hast kept my word and hast not denied my name.

Rev 3:10 because you have kept my word of patient endurance, *I will keep you from the hour of trial which is coming on the whole world, to try those who dwell upon the earth.*

To Laodicea's:

[Rev 3:16] so then because thou art lukewarm, and neither cold nor hot, I will spue thee out of my mouth. [Out into tribulation as in Rev. 2:22]

[Revelation 4:1] After this I looked, and, behold, *a door was opened in heaven*: and the first voice which I heard was as it were of a trumpet talking with me; which said, *come up hither,* and I will show thee things that must be hereafter.

[Rev 8:13] And I beheld, and heard an angel flying through the midst of heaven, saying with a loud voice, Woe, woe, woe, to the inhabiters of the earth [those not raptured?] by reason of the other voices of the trumpet of the three angels, which are yet to sound!

The feast of Trumpets (Open Door)

The Open Door and Last Trump are on the Feast of Trumpets, which is on the new moon. The new moon feast (holy day) is a shadow/prophesy of the Rapture. The open door is prominently seen in the rapture verses of Rev 3:10, 4:1 & Matt 25:1-13.

Col 2:16 Let no man therefore, judge you in meat, or in drink, or in respect of an *holyday* [festival], or of *the new moon*, or of the Sabbath days:

Col 2:17 Which *are a shadow of things to come*; but the body is of Christ.

Ezekiel 46:1 "Thus says the Lord GOD: The gate of the inner court that faces east shall be shut on the six working days; but on the Sabbath day it shall be opened and *on the day of the new moon it shall be opened.*

Ps 81:3 *Blow up the trumpet in the new moon*, in the time appointed, on our solemn feast day.

Isa 26:2 *Open ye the gates that the righteous nation which keepeth the truth may enter in.*

Ps 118:19 Open to me the gates of righteousness: I will go into them, and I will praise the LORD:

Ps 118:20 This gate of the LORD, into which the righteous shall enter.

John 10:7 then said Jesus unto them again, Verily, verily, I say unto you, I am the door of the sheep.

John 10:9 *I am the door*: by me if any man enter in, he shall be saved and shall go in and out, and find pasture.

Matthew 7:13 *Enter ye in at the strait gate*: for wide is the gate, and broad is the way, that leadeth to destruction, and many there be which go in thereat:

Matthew 7:14 Because strait is the *gate, and narrow is the way, which leadeth unto life*, and few there be that find it.

Luke 13:24 *Strive to enter in at the strait gate*: for many, I say unto you, will seek to enter in, and shall not be able.

Luke 13:25 When once the master of the house is risen up, and hath *shut to the door*, and ye begin to stand without, and to knock at the door, saying, Lord, Lord, open unto us; and he shall answer and say unto you, I know you not whence ye are:

The Feast of Trumpets, on the new moon, is *when the moon is turned to darkness*. It is also "*on a day or hour that no man knows*" -- which is an expression referring to this feast (and to a Jewish Wedding) -- because the new moon happens 29.5 days after the previous one, creating uncertainty of whether it will fall on the 29th or 30th day after the previous new moon, which is the first day of the month, thus the festival is traditionally celebrated for two days just to be sure.

Lev 23:24 Speak unto the children of Israel, saying, in the seventh month, in the first day of the month, shall ye have a Sabbath, a memorial of blowing of trumpets, and holy convocation.

Num 29:1 and in the seventh month, on the first day of the month, ye shall have a holy convocation; ye shall do no servile work: it is a day of blowing the trumpets unto you.

Just as the Lord Jesus Christ fulfilled all the spring feasts, and on each day of each feast, so too, will the fall feasts be fulfilled when Christ comes the second time, and in order and on each day of each feast. The Feast of Trumpets points to the rapture, the Day of Atonement points to Satan's defeat Tabernacles points to establishing the 1000-year kingdom. Trumpets are on the first, and Atonement is on the tenth. Excluding the days of the Festivals themselves, there are "seven days of Awe" or tribulation between them...Including, 10.

Rev 2:10 Fear none of those things which thou shalt suffer: behold, the devil shall cast some of you into prison, that ye may be tried; and *ye shall have tribulation ten days*: be thou faithful unto death, and I will give thee a crown of life.

2 Thess 2: Falling Away / Departure

All of the rapture positions (whether preterit, midrib, prewash, post rib) agrees that the rapture happens before the day of the Lord. In 2, Thessalonians 2, the false report that the Day of the Lord was present meant, therefore, that the resurrection and rapture (the departure) had come and gone and was in the past. That the resurrection was past was a common false report and is mentioned in 2 Timothy:

2 Tim 2:18 who concerning the truth have erred, saying that the resurrection is past already; and overthrow the faith of some.

Although the day of the Lord starts with the rapture, the *presence* of the Day of the Lord is wrath, darkness, trouble, and the tribulation. (Zephyr 1:15) The tribulations described in 2 Theses 1 were erroneously thought to be the tribulations of the day of the Lord.

2 Theses 2:1 now we beseech you, brethren, by the coming of our Lord Jesus Christ, and by our gathering together unto him, [rapture]

2 Theses 2:2 That ye be not soon shaken in mind, or be troubled, neither by spirit, nor by word, nor by letter as from us, as that the day of Christ [day of the Lord/tribulation] is at hand [present].

2 Theses 2:3 Let no man deceive you by any means: for that day [tribulation] shall not come [be present], except there comes a falling away [departure/rapture] first, and that man of sin be revealed, the son of perdition;

2 Theses 2:4 Who opposed and exalteth himself above all that is called God, or that is worshipped; so that he as God sitteth in the temple of God, shewing himself that he is God. 2 Thess 2:5 do you not remember that when I was still with you I told you this?

2 Thess 2:6 and now ye know what withholdeth that he might be revealed in his time.

2 Thess 2:7 for the mystery of iniquity doth already work: only he who now letteth will let, until he be taken out of the way. [The Church at the rapture]

2 Thess 2:8 and then shall that Wicked be revealed, whom the Lord shall consume with the spirit of his mouth, and shall destroy with the brightness of his coming:

In other words,

1.I beg you by our rapture hope,

2.That you don't worry if you hear that the Day of the Lord and the tribulation is present 3. (Don't be deceived)...Unless the departure (rapture) comes first, and the man of sin is revealed, the son of perdition

4. WHO will, (3.5 years later, according to Dan 9:27) sit in the temple as God, as the abomination of desolation Remember I told you this?

6. Now you know that it is your presence that withholds the man of sin, so that he will be revealed in due time.

7. For the antichrist is working now only a little, because we restrain him as we are here and pray, until the rapture, when we will be taken out of the way.

8. And then the antichrist will be revealed, whom the Lord will destroy with the arrival of his presence.

2 Thess 3:3 But the Lord is faithful, who shall establish you, and *keep you from evil.*

Jewish Wedding (*a theme of the Feast of Trumpets***)**

Bridal Chamber = Heaven

John 14:2 in my Father's house are many mansions: if it were not so, I would have told you. *I go to prepare a place for you.*

John 14:3 *And if I go and prepare a place for you, I will come again, and receive you unto myself; that where I am, there ye may be also.*

Our "many mansions" are in heaven (Rev 21:2). Jesus went away to heaven in Acts 1. The words in Italics above are an expression, used by the groom in a Jewish Wedding. A groom would say those words to his bride and then leave to build an addition onto his father's house before returning for his bride. He returns for his bride in the middle of the night, as a thief, at an hour she might not think, with a loud cry, and a procession of trumpet blast and his friends saying "Behold!
The Bridegroom Comes!" Entering our "bridal chamber/heavenly mansion" will be the start of the bridal week. This is shown in Isaiah and indicates that the tribulation will occur while we are "hid in the bridal chambers or heaven".

Isa 26:19 Thy *dead men shall live,* together with my dead body shall they arise. *Awake and sing,* ye that dwell in dust: for thy dew is as the dew of herbs, and the earth shall cast out the dead. Isa 26:20 *Come, my people, enter thou into thy chambers,* and shut *thy doors* about thee: *hide thyself* as it were for a little moment *until the indignation be overpast.*

Isa 26:21 for, behold the LORD cometh out of his place to punish the inhabitants of the earth for their iniquity: the earth also shall disclose her blood and shall no more cover her slain.

Being "hid in the Lord's house, or heaven during tribulation" is also seen in Psalm 27, which is to be read daily in the 30 days prior to the Feast of Trumpets.

Ps 27:4 One thing have I desired of the LORD, that will I seek after; that I may *dwell in the house of the LORD* all the days of my life, to behold the beauty of the LORD and to enquire in his temple. Ps 27:5 for *in the time of trouble* he shall *hide me in his pavilion*: in the secret of his tabernacle shall he *hide me*; he shall set me up upon a rock.

Ps 27:6 and now shall *mine head be lifted up* above mine enemies round about me: therefore, will I offer in his tabernacle sacrifices of joy; I will sing, yea, I will sing praises unto the LORD.

Hiding, being hid, having a place to hide away are themes of being hidden away in the bridal chamber during the wedding, as we will be hidden in heaven during the tribulation.

Zeph 2:3 Seek ye the LORD, all ye meek of the earth, which have wrought his judgment; seek righteousness, seek meekness: *it may be ye shall be hid in the day of the LORD's anger.*

The Church is the Bride of Christ.

Eph 5:25 Husbands, love your wives, even as Christ also loved the church, and gave himself for it;

Eph 5:31 For this cause shall a man leave his father and mother, and shall be joined unto his wife, and they two shall be one flesh.

Eph 5:32 this is a great mystery: but I speak concerning Christ and the church.

2Cor 11:2 for I am jealous over you with godly jealousy: for I have espoused you to one husband that I may present you as a chaste virgin to Christ.

The Rapture is likened to a wedding, and from the Bible, we know a wedding lasts a week, we know the rapture will be pre-tribulation. The scriptures define a marriage as being a weeklong event. (Bridal week) = (Tribulation week)

Judges 14:1-18...And Samson made a *feast there, as was customary for bridegrooms.* ...If you can give me the answer within *the seven days of the feast...* She cried the whole *seven days of the feast*.

Genesis 29:22-28 So Laban brought together all the people of the place and gave a feast. ...Finish this daughter's *bridal week*

The time of intimacy (the bride being with the bridegroom sealed away in the bridal chamber) begins at the start of the bridal week, and this is what we look forward to in the pre-tribulation rapture.

The Parable of the 10 virgins contains many themes of the rapture, the marriage, and the feast of trumpets.

[Mat 25:1] Then shall the kingdom of heaven be likened unto ten virgins, which took their lamps and went forth to meet the bridegroom.

[Mat 25:2] And five of them were wise, and five were foolish.

[Mat 25:3] They that were foolish took their lamps and took no oil with them:

[Mat 25:4] But the wise took oil in their vessels with their lamps.

[Mat 25:5] While the bridegroom tarried, they all *slumbered and slept.*

[Mat 25:6] And at midnight there was a cry made, *Behold, the bridegroom cometh*; go ye out to meet him.

[Mat 25:7] Then all those virgins arose, and trimmed their lamps.

[Mat 25:8] And the foolish said unto the wise, give us of your oil; for our lamps are gone out. [Mat 25:9] But the wise answered, saying, not so; lest there be not enough for us and you: but go ye rather to them that sell, and buy for yourselves.

[Mat 25:10] And while they went to buy, the bridegroom came, and *they that were ready went in with him to the marriage*: and *the door was shut.*

[Mat 25:11] Afterward came also the other virgins, saying, Lord, Lord, open to us.

[Mat 25:12] But he answered and said, Verily I say unto you, I know you not.

[Mat 25:13] *Watch therefore, for ye know neither the day nor the hour* wherein the Son of man cometh.

At the end of the tribulation, people are in heaven (the bride, the Church), and coming down out of heaven, because they have been there for 7 years.

[Luke 12:36] And ye yourselves like unto men that wait for their lord, when **he will return from the wedding**; that when he cometh and knocked, they may open unto him immediately.

[Rev 19:1] And after these things I heard a great voice of much **people in heaven** [the raptured], saying, Alleluia; Salvation, and glory, and honor, and power, unto the Lord our God:

[Rev 19:7] Let us rejoice and exult and give him the glory, for **the marriage of the Lamb has come**, and his Bride has made herself ready;

[Rev 19:8] it was granted her to be clothed with fine linen, bright and pure"--for the fine linen is the righteous deeds of the saints.

[Rev 19:9] And the angel said to me, "Write this: Blessed are those who are invited to **the marriage supper of the Lamb**." And he said to me, "These are true words of God."

[Rev 19:14] And **the armies which were in heaven followed him** [the raptured] upon white horses, clothed in fine linen, white and clean.

[Mat 24:29] Immediately **after the tribulation** of those days shall the sun be darkened, and the moon shall not give her light, and the stars shall fall from heaven, and the powers of the heavens shall be shaken:

[Mat 24:30] And then shall appear the sign of the Son of man in heaven: and then shall all the tribes of the earth mourn, and they shall see the Son of man coming in the clouds of heaven with power and great glory.

[Mat 24:31] And he shall send his angels with a great sound of a trumpet, and they shall gather together his elect from the four winds, **from one end of heaven** to the other.

[Zech 14:5] And ye shall flee to the valley of the mountains; for the valley of the mountains shall reach unto Azal: yea, ye shall flee, like as ye fled from before the earthquake in the days of Uzziah king of Judah: and **the LORD my God shall come, and all the saints with thee.**

[Jud 1:14] And Enoch also, the seventh from Adam, prophesied of these, saying, Behold, **the Lord cometh with ten thousands of his saints,**

[Col 3:4] When Christ, who is our life, shall appear, **then** shall ye also appear with him in glory?

Interesting verse number: 12:12 12 is written all over New Jerusalem, and there are 24 elders in heaven after the rapture in Rev. 4:1.

[Rev 12:12] **Rejoice then, O heaven and you that dwell therein**! But woe to you, O earth and sea, for the devil has come down to you in great wrath, because he knows that his time is short!" Yes, the Bride is in heaven, coming down out of heaven at the end of the tribulation:

[Rev 21:2] And I John saw the holy city, New Jerusalem, **coming down from God out of heaven, prepared as a bride adorned for her husband.**

[Rev 21:9] And there came unto me one of the seven angels which had the seven vials full of the seven last plagues, and talked with me, saying, **Come hither, I will show thee the bride, the Lamb's wife.**

[Rev 21:10] And he carried me away in the spirit to a great and high mountain, and **shewed me that great city, the holy Jerusalem, descending out of heaven from God,** Mt. Zion & New Jerusalem: God's bride.

[Heb 12:22] But ye are come unto *mount Sion*, and unto the city of the living God, the *heavenly Jerusalem*, and to an innumerable company of angels,

[Isa 51:16] And I have put my words in thy mouth, and I have covered thee in the shadow of mine hand, that I may plant the heavens, and lay the foundations of the earth, and say unto *Zion, Thou art my people.*

Daniel's 70th Week

The 70th week of Daniel, which becomes the 7-year Tribulation, is a judgment and curse determined upon Isreal, not the Church.

Dan 9:24 Seventy weeks are *determined upon thy people* and upon thy holy city, to finish the transgression, and to make an end of sins, and to make reconciliation for iniquity, and to bring in everlasting righteousness, and to seal up the vision and prophecy, and to anoint the most Holy. Dan 9:25 Know therefore and understand, that from the going forth of the commandment to restore and to build Jerusalem unto the Messiah the Prince shall be seven weeks, and threescore and two weeks: the street shall be built again, and the wall, even in troublous times.

Dan 9:26 And after threescore and two weeks shall Messiah be cut off, but not for himself: and the people of the prince that shall come shall destroy the city and the sanctuary; and the end thereof shall be with a flood, and unto the end of the war desolations are determined.

Dan 9:27 And **he shall confirm the covenant with many for one week**: and **in the midst of the week** he shall cause the sacrifice and the oblation to cease, and for the overspreading of **abominations he shall make it desolate**, even until the consummation, and that determined shall be poured upon the desolate.

The Church's sins are taken care of by Jesus' death, and we are not under the curse of the law, nor is the 70th week "to make an end for sins" determined for the Church.

[Gal 3:13] **Christ hath redeemed us from the curse of the law**, being made a curse for us: for it is written, Cursed is every one that hangeth on a tree:

[Gal 5:18] But if ye be led of the Spirit, **ye are not under the law.**

[Rom 6:14] For sin shall not have dominion over you: for **ye are not under the law**, but under grace.

[1Cor 6:12] **All things are lawful unto me**, but all things are not expedient: all things are lawful for me, but **I will not be brought under the power of any.**

There is no need for the tribulation to purge or cleanse the Church. The blood of Christ, and the Word of God, sanctifies and cleans the Church, and makes us spotless, and ready for the rapture now.

Hebrews 13:12 Wherefore Jesus also, that he might sanctify the people with his own blood, suffered without the gate.

1John 1:7 But if we walk in the light, as he is in the light, we have fellowship one with another, and the blood of Jesus Christ his Son cleanseth us from all sin.

Eph 5:26 That he might sanctify and cleanse it with the washing of water by the word, Eph 5:27 That he might present it to himself a glorious church, not having spot, or wrinkle, or any such thing; but that it should be holy and without blemish.

Who has dominion?
Satan or the Lord Jesus Christ's Church?

Satan will be given dominion for 42 months on earth, the second half of Daniel's 70th week, and the Church will not be put under Satan's dominion. The Church, given power by the Almighty Father in heaven, in the name of the Lord Jesus Christ, by the power of the Holy Spirit, restrains Satan, as was shown in 2 Thess 2. We know that Satan has not had full dominion over the Church, even though there are many Christian brothers dying still today, for if Satan did have this power, the Word of God would have been extinguished from the face of the earth by now. History alone proves that the Church is more powerful than Satan in this age, but the scriptures speak for themselves:

[Mark 3:14] And he ordained twelve, that they should be with him, and that he might send them forth to preach,

[Mark 3:15] And to have power to heal sicknesses, and **to cast out devils**:

[Mark 6:7] And he called unto him the twelve, and began to send them forth by two and two; and **gave them power over unclean spirits**;

[Mark 6:13.4] **And they cast out many devils**, and anointed with oil many that were sick, and healed them.

[Luke 9:1] Then he called his twelve disciples together, and **gave them power and authority over all devils**, and to cure diseases.

[Luke 10:19] Behold, I **give unto you power to tread on serpents and scorpions, and over all the power of the enemy**: and nothing shall by any means hurt you.

[Mat 10:8] Heal the sick, cleanse the lepers, **raise the dead, cast out devils**: freely ye have received, freely give.

Casting out Devils was not "just for the disciples only". Anyone can do this in the name of the Lord Jesus Christ. [Mark 9:38.11] And John answered him, saying, **Master, we saw one casting out devils in thy name, and he followeth not us**: and we forbad him, because he followeth not us.

[Mark 9:39] But Jesus said, Forbid him not: for there is no man which shall do a miracle in my name, that can lightly speak evil of me.

[Mark 9:40] For he that is not against us is on our part.

Successfully casting out devils, does not make one "saved". Hence, if "unsaved" can cast out devils, then the Church surely has the power to restrain Satan.

Mat 7:21 Not every one that saith unto me, Lord, Lord, shall enter into the kingdom of heaven; but he that doeth the will of my Father which is in heaven.

Mat 7:22 Many will say to me in that day, Lord, Lord, have we not prophesied in thy name? and in thy name have cast out devils? and in thy name done many wonderful works?

Mat 7:23 And then will I profess unto them, I never knew you: depart from me, ye that work iniquity.

Eph 6:12 For **we wrestle** not against flesh and blood, but against principalities, against powers, against the rulers of the darkness of this world, **against spiritual wickedness in high places.**

Mat 16:19 And I will give unto thee the keys of the kingdom of heaven: and **whatsoever thou shalt bind on**

earth shall be bound in heaven: and whatsoever thou shalt loose on earth shall be loosed in heaven.

Mat 16:18 And I say also unto thee, That thou art Peter, and upon this rock **I will build my church, and the gates of hell shall not prevail against it.**

But Satan will be given dominion and power to dominate the other way around!

Dan 7:21 I beheld, and the same horn made **war with the saints and prevailed against them;**

Rev 13:7 And it was given unto him to make **war with the saints and to overcome them: and power was given him over all kindreds, and tongues, and nations.**

So the Church must be raptured, "caught up", & Satan fights whoever is left over, the tribulation saints; those of the 7 churches who were spewed out into the time of testing, and repent and keep the commandments, and those foolish virgins in Matthew 25 who were expecting Christ's return, but were too busy with the world and caught unprepared.

The man child ruler Raptured in Rev 12

...is Christ and the Church (Christ is the head, the Church is the Body)

The woman giving birth is not the Bride. Jesus comes for a virgin bride. The woman is Isreal (who gave birth to Christ and Christians), who Satan turns to persecute after the rapture. But she is protected by God, so Satan turns toward new believers who are the "remnant of her seed" -- tribulation saints, people repent in the tribulation, after the rapture. The man child, the woman's first child, which is caught up [harpazo] to God, is the Church in the pretribulation rapture.

Rev 12:4 And his tail drew the third part of the stars of heaven and did cast them to the earth: and the dragon stood before the woman which was ready to be delivered, for to devour her child as soon as it was born.

Rev 12:5 And she brought forth *a man child, who was to rule all nations with a rod of iron: and her child was caught up unto God and to his throne.*

All three characteristics of the man child (1, *ruling over the nations,* 2, *with a rod of iron,* 3 *sitting on his throne),* apply to both Christ AND the Church. Christ rules, and we rule as his bride:

Rev 2:26 He who conquers and who keeps my works until the end, *I will give him power over the nations,*

Rev 2:27 *and he shall rule them with a rod of iron,* as when earthen pots are broken in pieces, even as I myself have received power from my Father;

Rev 5:10 And hast made us unto our God kings and priests: and *we shall reign* on the earth. Rev 3:21 To him that overcometh will I grant *to sit with me in my throne,* even as I also overcame, and am set down with my Father in his throne.

That these characteristics apply to the Church, and that the man child represents the Church does not deny that the man child is Christ. Christ is an essential part of the Church, the HEAD!

Col 1:18 And *he is the head of the body, the church*: who is the beginning, the firstborn from the dead; that in all things he might have the preeminence.

Since the other "seed" of the woman represents believers (Saints of the Tribulation), the man child also represents the many believers of the Church.

Rev 12:17 And the dragon was wroth with the woman, and went to make war with *the remnant of her seed,* which keep the commandments of God, and have the testimony of Jesus Christ.

The man child nation is delivered or caught up to God, before the travail, (the time of trouble, the tribulation, the Day of the Lord).

Isa 66:7 *Before she travailed,* she brought forth; before her pain came, *she was delivered of a man child.*

8 Who hath heard such a thing? Who hath seen such things? Shall the earth be made to bring forth in one day? Or shall a *nation* be born at once? For as soon as Zion travailed, she brought forth *her children.*

9 Shall I bring to the birth, and not cause to bring forth? saith the LORD: shall I cause to bring forth, and shut the womb? saith thy God.

Christianity is a "nation".

1 Peter 2:9 But *ye are a chosen generation, a royal priesthood, an holy nation,* a peculiar people; that ye should shew forth the praises of him who hath called you *out of darkness into his marvellous light;*

"Lights/Christians" are not in "Darkness/Day of Lord/tribulation!"

[Mat 5:14] *Ye are the light* of the world. A city that is set on an hill cannot be hid.

[Phil 2:15] That ye may be blameless and harmless, the sons of God, without rebuke, in the midst of a crooked and perverse nation, among whom ye shine as lights in the world;

[John 8:12] Then spake Jesus again unto them, saying, I am the light of the world: *he that followeth me shall not walk in darkness,* but shall have the light of life.

[Amos 5:18] Woe unto you that desire the day of the LORD! to what end is it for you? *the day of the LORD is darkness,* and not light.

[Amos 5:20] Shall not the day of the LORD be darkness, and not light? even very dark, and no brightness in it?

[Joel 2:1] Blow ye the trumpet in Zion, and sound an alarm in my holy mountain: let all the inhabitants of the land tremble: for the *day of the LORD* cometh, for it is nigh at hand; [Joel 2:2] *A day of darkness and of gloominess, a day of clouds and of thick darkness,* as the morning spread upon the mountains: a great people and a strong; there hath not been ever the like, neither shall be any more after it, even to the years of many generations.

[Joel 2:31] The sun shall be turned into darkness, and the moon into blood, before the great and terrible day of the LORD come.

[Mat 24:21] For then shall be great tribulation, such as was not since the beginning of the world to this time, no, nor ever shall be.

[Zeph 1:15] *That day is a day of wrath, a day of trouble and distress, a day of wasteness and desolation, a day of darkness and gloominess, a day of clouds and thick darkness,*

[1Thess 5:4] *But ye, brethren, are not in darkness,* that that day should overtake you as a thief. [1Thess 5:5] *Ye are all the children of light,* and the children of the day: we are not of the night, nor of darkness.

[Col 1:12] Giving thanks unto the Father, which hath made us meet to be partakers of the inheritance of the saints in light: [Col 1:13] Who hath delivered us from the power of darkness, and hath translated us into the kingdom of his dear Son:

So, another reason why Christians of the present age are not in that darkness, when Satan will have dominion, is:

[Mat 12:25] And Jesus knew their thoughts, and said unto them, every kingdom divided against itself is brought to desolation; and every city or house divided against itself shall not stand: [Mark 3:24] And if a kingdom be divided against itself, that kingdom cannot stand.

We cannot effectively pray against Satan taking power, when God gives Satan power. It will be tough for the tribulation saints, God, let them be killed.

[Rev 13:10] He that leadeth into captivity shall go into captivity: he that killeth with the sword must be killed with the sword. Here is the patience and the faith of the saints.

[Rev 14:12] Here is the patience of the saints: here are they that keep the commandments of God, and the faith of Jesus.

[Rev 14:13] And I heard a voice from heaven saying unto me, Write, Blessed are the dead which die in the Lord from henceforth: Yea, saith the Spirit, that they may rest from their labours; and their works do follow them.

Noah and Lot as examples of deliverance!

The Rapture is compared to Noah's and Lot's time when people are caught unaware going about their daily lives. Peter describes Noah and Lot as examples of the rapture, stressing deliverance.

2Pet 2:4 For if God spared not the angels that sinned, but cast them down to hell, and delivered them into chains of darkness, to be reserved unto judgment;

2Pet 2:5 And spared not the old world, but *saved Noah* the eighth person, a preacher of righteousness, bringing in the flood upon the world of the ungodly;

2Pet 2:6 And turning the cities of Sodom and Gomorrha into ashes condemned them with an overthrow, making them an ensample unto those that after should live ungodly; 2Pet 2:7 And *delivered just Lot,* vexed with the filthy conversation of the wicked: 2Pet 2:8 (For that righteous man dwelling among them, in seeing and hearing, vexed his righteous soul from day to day with their unlawful deeds;)

2Pet 2:9 *The Lord knoweth how to deliver the godly out of temptations* and to reserve the unjust unto *the day of judgment* to be punished:

(The Day of Judgment is the day of the Lord, the time of trouble, the tribulation, the time of wrath, the time of testing, the time of temptation.)

Luke 17:26 And as it was in the days of **Noah**, so shall it be also in the days of the Son of man. Luke 17:27 *They did eat,* *they drank, they married wives, they were given in marriage,* until the day that Noah entered into the ark, and the flood came, and destroyed them all.

Luke 17:28 Likewise also as it was in the days of Lot; they did eat, they drank, they bought, they sold, they planted, they builded;

Luke 17:29 But the same day that Lot went out of Sodom it rained fire and brimstone from heaven, and destroyed them all.

Matthew 24:36 But of that day and hour knoweth no man, no, not the angels of heaven, but my Father only.

Matthew 24:37 But as the days of Noah were, so shall also the coming of the Son of man be.

Matthew 24:38 For *as in the days that were before the flood they were eating and drinking, marrying and giving in marriage,* until the day that Noah entered into the ark,

Matthew 24:39 And knew not until the flood came and took them all away; so shall also the coming of the Son of man be.

The wicked people will be taking no notice, eating and drinking, before the rapture happens. People eating, drinking, and feasting at marriage parties does not describe the tribulation, when famine will come upon the earth. See Rev 6:5-8, 18:8

One taken (in the rapture); the other left (behind in tribulation).

Matthew 24:40 Then shall two be in the field; the one shall be taken, and the other left. Matthew 24:41 Two women shall be grinding at the mill; the one shall be taken, and the other left.

Luke 17:33 Whosoever shall seek to save his life shall lose it and whosoever shall lose his life shall preserve it.

Luke 17:34 I tell you, in that night there shall be two men in one bed; the one shall be taken, and the other shall be left.

Luke 17:35 Two women shall be grinding together; the one shall be taken, and the other left.

Luke 17:36 Two men shall be in the field; the one shall be taken, and the other left.

Gathered to the body of the Lord, as Eagles

Luke 17:37 And they answered and said unto him, Where, Lord? And he said unto them, wheresoever the body is, thither will the eagles be gathered together.

Mat 24:28 For wheresoever the carcase is, there will the eagles be gathered together.

Isa 40:31 But they that wait upon the LORD shall renew their strength; they *shall mount up with wings as eagles;* they shall run, and not be weary, and they shall walk, and not faint.

Joh 6:53 Then Jesus said unto them, Verily, verily, I say unto you, *Except ye eat the flesh of the Son of man,* and drink his blood, ye have no life in you.

Mark 13:27 And then shall he send his angels, and shall gather together his elect from the four winds, from the uttermost part of the earth to the uttermost part of heaven.

Not knowing the day or the hour.

The Feast of Trumpets happens on the "new moon", which is 29.5 days after the last one, meaning it might

Occur on the 29th or 30th day, nobody knows for sure. "Of that day or hour no man knows" is an expression referring to this feast, and thus, the rapture.

"Of that day or hour no man knows, but my Father only" is an expression used by a groom when asked when he will go and steal away his bride like a thief in the night. He says this because it is his Father that will tell him when his preparations on the bridal chamber are completed, and it is time.

Since the Feast of Trumpets is the "wedding of the Messiah", then this expression about "not knowing the day or the hour" refers to the rapture, and means that the rapture must take place on a Feast of Trumpets.

Matthew 24:36 But of that day and hour knoweth no man, no, not the angels of heaven, but my Father only.

Matthew 24:42 Watch therefore: for ye know not what hour your Lord doth come.

Matthew 25:13 Watch therefore, for ye know neither the day nor the hour wherein the Son of man cometh.

Mar 13:32 But of that day and that hour knoweth no man, no, not the angels which are in heaven, neither the Son, but the Father.

Mar 13:33 Take ye heed, watch and pray: for ye know not when the time is.

Mar 13:34 For the Son of Man is as a man taking a far journey, who left his house, and gave authority to his servants, and to every man his work, and commanded the porter to watch. Mar 13:35 Watch ye therefore: for ye know not when the master of the house cometh, at even, or at midnight, or at the cockcrowing, or in the morning:

Mar 13:36 Lest coming suddenly he find you sleeping.

Mar 13:37 And what I say unto you I say unto all, Watch.

Thus, not knowing the day or the hour *is a parable*, and, as all parables, is designed to prevent unbelievers from understanding the meaning. See Matthew 13:10-17.

The reality is that believers WILL and CAN know the time, because this phrase indicates the Feast of Trumpets.

Other verses on this topic plainly declare that *not knowing* is a punishment for the wicked servant:

Mat 24:48 But and if that evil servant shall say in his heart, My lord delayeth his coming;

Mat 24:49 And shall begin to smite his fellow-servants, and to eat and drink with the drunken; Mat 24:50 The lord of that servant shall come in a day when he looketh not for him, and in an hour that he is not aware of,

Mat 24:51 And shall cut him asunder, and appoint him his portion with the hypocrites: there shall be weeping and gnashing of teeth.

Luke 12:45 But and if that servant say in his heart, My lord delayeth his coming; and shall begin to beat the menservants and maidens, and to eat and drink, and to be drunken;

Luke 12:46 The lord of that servant will come in a day when he looketh not for him, and at an hour when he is not aware, and will cut him in sunder, and will appoint him his portion with the unbelievers.

Rev 3:3 Remember therefore how thou hast received and heard, and hold fast, and repent. If therefore thou shalt not watch, I will come on thee as a thief, and thou shalt not know what hour I will come upon thee.

Since "not knowing what hour" is the punishment for not watching and a punishment for the unfaithful servant, it does not apply to faithful believers. And other scriptures confirm that we will know the hour:

1Th 5:1 But of the times and the seasons, brethren, *ye have no need that I write unto you.*

1Th 5:2 *For yourselves know perfectly* that the *day of the Lord so cometh as a thief in the night*. 1Th 5:3 For when they shall say, Peace and safety; then sudden destruction cometh upon them, as travail upon a woman with child; and they shall not escape. 1Th 5:4 But *ye, brethren, are not in darkness, that that day should overtake you as a thief.* 1Th 5:5 Ye *are all the children of light,* and the children of the day: we are not of the night, nor of darkness.

1Th 5:6 Therefore let us not sleep, as do others; but *let us watch* and be sober.

1Th 5:7 For they that sleep sleep in the night; and they that be drunken are drunken in the night. 1Th 5:8 But let us, who are of the day, be sober, putting on the breastplate of faith and love; and for an helmet, the hope of salvation.

1Th 5:9 For God hath not appointed us to wrath, but to obtain salvation by our Lord Jesus Christ,

The Lord comes for his bride as a thief in the night to take her away in the marriage.

1Th 5:2 For yourselves know perfectly that the *day of the Lord so cometh as a thief in the night.*

Matthew 24:43 But know this, that if the goodman of the house had known in what watch the thief would come, he would have watched, and would not have suffered his house to be broken up.

Matthew 24:44 Therefore be ye also ready: for in such an hour as ye think not the Son of man cometh.

Luke 12:37 Blessed are those servants, *whom the lord when he cometh shall find watching*: verily I say unto you, that he shall gird himself, and make them to sit down to meat, and will come forth and serve them.

Luke 12:38 And if he shall come in the second watch, or come in the third watch, and find them so, blessed are those servants.

Luk 12:39 And this know, that if the good man of the house had known what hour the thief would come, *he would have watched,* and not have suffered his house to be broken through. Luke 12:40 Be ye therefore ready also: for the Son of man cometh at an hour when ye think not.

Because the "day or hour no man knows" refers to the marriage at the Feast of Trumpets, and because not knowing is a punishment for the evil servant, and because we are too "know perfectly", and because "we are not in darkness", then we can watch and be ready, because we DO KNOW when the thief will come. Like the good man of the house, we should "be therefore ready".

Those who deny the pretribulation rapture are like the evil servant, they say something else; they say the master will delay his coming until after the tribulation. (Luke 12:45, Mat 24:48) and they are NOT watching for him now (Rev 3:3).

John 10:10 The thief cometh not, but for to steal, and to kill, and to destroy: *I am come that they might have life and that they might have it more abundantly.*

Rev 16:15 *Behold, I come as a thief. Blessed is he that watcheth,* and keepeth his garments, lest he walk naked, and they see his shame.

We look forward to Christ's appearing and return.

Will Christians REALLY be spared the Tribulation?

[Ps 97:10] Ye that love the LORD, hate evil: *he preserveth the souls of his saints; he delivereth them out of the hand of the wicked.*

[Rom 5:8] But God commendeth his love toward us, in that, while we were yet sinners, Christ died for us.

[Rom 5:9] Much more then, being now justified by his blood, **we shall be saved from wrath through him**.

[Rom 5:10] For if, when we were enemies, we were reconciled to God by the death of his Son, **much more, being reconciled, we shall be saved** by his life.

[Isa 57:1] The righteous *perisheth,* and no man layeth it to heart: and *merciful men are taken away,* none considering that the righteous is *taken away from the evil to come.*

Mic 7:2 *The good man is perished out of the earth*: and there is none upright among men: they all lie in wait for blood; they hunt every man his brother with a net.

[Mal 3:16] Then they that feared the LORD spake often one to another: and the LORD hearkened, and heard it, and a book of remembrance was written before him for them that feared the LORD, and that thought upon his name.

[Mal 3:17] And they shall be mine, saith the LORD of hosts, *in that day when I make up my jewels*; and *I will spare them, as a man spareth his own son that serveth him.*

[Mal 3:18] Then shall ye return, and discern between the righteous and the wicked, between him that serveth God and him that serveth him not.

[Mal 4:1] For, behold, the day cometh, that shall burn as an oven; and all the proud, yea, and all that do wickedly, shall be stubble: and *the day that cometh shall burn them up,* saith the LORD of hosts, that it shall leave them neither root nor branch.

[2Tim 4:18] And *the Lord shall deliver me from every evil work, and will preserve me unto his heavenly kingdom*: to whom be glory for ever and ever. Amen.

Close chatters, life matters

Who knows?

My mind's gone

As I sit disturbed and bent

My mind drifts, don't trip

My wires might cross

Too old to be mad

Too mad to be old

Therefore, my mental start working

The unborn rage

The fragment Of what's left

To the dead white cells

My ego goes tick

My bells go pop

It's a human virus

Given by man

Created by man

To destroy all

But the rage can't consume me

Its secret can't hold me It's the beast within.

Let Me Be

They say I'm old

It's my age

They claim I'm crazy

It's my mind

They say it's gone

I drift in and out

They flash in

They flash out

Things I don't forget about.

Soda pops

And gumball drops

They say I'm crazy

I say its age

Dreaming of yester years

Old school dance

And big boy bands

Doo –Wops

And lollipops

The year 1957

Felt like heaven

Boy and girl groups

One cent jukes

My mind drifts

Because I'm alone

Stuck in this

Old folks home

No family no friends

Just wondering

When will it end?

So let me be

SD - #0025 - 070726 - C0 - 234/156/6 - PB - 9780692659014 - Gloss Lamination